GENESIS
AND *GENDER*

Biblical Myths of Sexuality and Their Cultural Impact

William E. Phipps

PRAEGER

New York
Westport, Connecticut
London

Library of Congress Cataloging-in-Publication Data

Phipps, William E., 1930-
    Genesis and gender: Biblical myths of sexuality and their cultural
impact/William E. Phipps.
        p. cm.
    Bibliography: p.
    Includes index.
    ISBN 0-275-93200-1
    1. Sex role — Biblical teaching. 2. Sex — Biblical teaching. 3. Creation —
Biblical teaching. 4. Bible. O.T. Genesis — Criticism, interpretation, etc. 5.
Bible — Criticism, interpretation, etc. 6. Myth in the Bible. I. Title.
BS652.P55 1989
220.8'3053 — dc 19   88-27509

Library of Congress Catalog Card Number: 88-27509
ISBN: 0-275-93200-1

First published in 1989

Praeger Publishers, One Madison Avenue, New York, NY 10010
A division of Greenwood Press, Inc.

Printed in the United States of America

The paper used in this book complies with the Permanent Paper Standard
issued by the National Information Standards Organization (Z39.48-1984).

10 9 8 7 6 5 4 3 2 1

To Catherine Mason Swezey

*in whose personality the qualities of Martha and Mary
are blended. In her active role Mama has been
a suffragette, an investor, and a homemaker.
In her contemplative role she has been a painter,
a student of religious anthropology,
and a listener to nine grandchildren.*

Contents

Introduction: The Purpose of Myths

This book is about the most influential myths ever told and their significance for resolving some long-standing gender problems. The creation stories of Genesis are of central importance in Judaism, Christianity, and Islam. Being the source of revelatory life-styles and authoritative doctrines, the myths have continually been transmitted by the religious faithful. They have also had an impact on those whose orientation is secular. However, crucial points pertaining to gender have generally been missed because faulty traditional interpretations have been accepted uncritically.

Before a discussion of biblical texts and interpretations can properly get underway in the following chapters, a semantic confusion must be addressed. The term *myth* has provoked much controversy because it has at least two basic meanings in the original Greek and in other European languages. Both meanings share the awareness that myths are fictions. The significant difference in this: in popular talk myths are false fictions, but in scholarly talk myths are true fictions.

In common parlance a myth refers to a fabrication which ignorant people accept as true. For example, one "myth" about pregnancy is that it can be prevented by having intercourse while standing. Politicians sometimes prefer the soft word "myth" to the libelous word "lie" in referring to their opponents' positions. *Old Myths and New Realities*, the title of Senator Fulbright's book about government policies, suggests

that myths are unreal outlooks which citizens should discard.[1]
Some second-century Christians denounced as myths those
Gnostic accounts which denied what was clearly observable.
Second Peter, for example, states: "We did not follow cunningly
devised myths [Greek, *muthoi*] when we made known to you
the power and coming of our Lord Jesus Christ, but we were
eyewitnesses of his majesty."[2]

In contrast to prevailing derogatory connotations, myth as
used by critical thinkers from the ancient Greeks onward connotes a story about divine-human relationships which provides
insight into the way things are or should be. Plato, for example,
used *muthos* to refer to his literary creations which pointed to
metaphysical realities. Philosopher W. T. Jones observes:

> Plato thought that none of the really important things —
> the real essence of goodness, nobility of spirit, humanity —
> could be condensed into neat copybook maxims. They
> elude these as the real flavor of Paris eludes a Baedeker
> guidebook. . . . To those who are not fortunate enough to
> participate in such an experience directly Plato offered a
> *myth*, which is, as it were, an imitation of the experience.
> . . . It is not a fairy tale designed to amuse; it says in the
> language of poetry and art what is too subtle and elusive
> to be said in any other way.[3]

Although an intellectual of the first order, Plato was convinced
that vivid symbolic tales, fictitious though they be, can disclose
truth unfathomed by the ordinary methods of logical discourse.
His myth of the cave, for instance, has probably provided more
insight into the purposes of liberal education than any essay ever
written. Likewise, his androgyne myth sheds considerable light, as
we shall see, on human sexuality. Thus myths thrust persons
beyond abstract concepts and scientific analysis and enable them
to obtain a synoptic vision on matters of fundamental importance.

In Western Asia, myth was esteemed as much as in the
Greek culture and for much the same reason. Cornelius
Loew states:

Myth was the special language form through which basic convictions were expressed in the ancient Near Eastern cultures. . . . As the story was recited . . . the human and the divine, the mortal and the immortal, the secular and the sacred coalesced *here and now* for those who experienced the ultimate reality of which the myth spoke.[4]

Ancient cultures did not treat myths as matter-of-fact history but valued them as imaginative treatments of abiding concerns. In this regard a paradox of Roman essayist Sallust is illuminating: "A myth has never happened but it happens every day." A myth is valued and continued in a culture if it deals with daily existential situations. Regarding ancient categories of reality, Brevard Childs writes:

There is no actual distinction in mythical time between the past, the present, and the future. Although the origin of time is projected into the past, to the primeval act of becoming, this is only a form in which an essentially timeless reality is clothed. Time is always present and yet to come.[5]

Myth is an expression of art, not science. Painters use their brushes to convey a dimension of depth, even though such cannot literally be accomplished on a flat surface. Likewise, literary artists with religious convictions use story forms to convey their perspectives on the Eternal's interaction with the temporal scene. Myths are their vehicle for transcending mundane reality and envisioning what is at least as true as descriptive accounts of nature. Most people do not or cannot take advantage of the experience of viewing art masterpieces directly and are thereby limited to looking at reproductions of varying faithfulness to the original. In a parallel manner, many know about myths only through the perverting glosses of subsequent interpreters.

The creation stories of the Hebrews and of other peoples are myths in the scholarly sense of the word. They abound in religion traditions as ways of expressing matters of ultimate significance. Many of these creation myths draw analogies from ceramics, one of the oldest technologies. A common presumption is that a transcendent power has formed physical things in a manner similar to the way potters make clay figurines and utensils. But unlike human potters, the divine Potter has a means for transferring life to forms.

Selected to illustrate the ceramic metaphor are myths from two widely differing geographical areas:

> The Maoris of New Zealand say that a certain god . . . took red riverside clay, kneaded it with his own blood into a likeness or image of himself, with eyes, legs, arms, and all complete, in fact, an exact copy of the deity; and having perfected the model, he animated it by breathing into its mouth and nostrils, whereupon the clay effigy at once came to life and sneezed. . . . So like himself was the man whom the Maori Creator Tiki fashioned that he called him *Tiki-ahua*, that is Tiki's likeness.
>
> The Ewe-speaking tribes of Togo-land, in West Africa, think that God still makes men out of clay. When a little of the water with which he moistens the clay remains over, he pours it on the ground, and out of that he makes the bad and disobedient people. When he wishes to make a good man he makes him out of good clay; but when he wishes to make a bad man, he employs only bad clay for the purpose. In the beginning God fashioned a man and set him on the earth; after that he fashioned a woman. The two looked at each other and began to laugh, whereupon God sent them into the world.[6]

In comparison with myths that anthropologists have gathered from other simple cultures, the Hebrew creation myths display both similarities and differences. By way of introducing these myths—which constitute only a small portion of biblical literature—it should be observed that Hebrew mythmakers wished to be taken seriously but not literally. They no more thought snakes actually had theological doubts and spoke human language than did the ancient fable-writer Aesop believe donkeys could think and converse like humans. The Hebrews believed in a nonphysical God,[7] so anthropomorphic references to God working with mud and walking about in Eden were intended to have symbolic meaning. Also, temporal sequence — so essential to scientific truth — is irrelevant in myths. In one creation myth of Genesis, for example, wild animals are created before humans and in another they are created after humans.

To assume that the Genesis mythmakers were attempting to state something about the process of historical development is to myth-understand! Due to scientific reductionism which equates the totality of reality with the observable and measurable, the presumption has arisen that creation accounts are either historical descriptions or worthless superstitions. The controversy might be compared to a foolish argument over whether there are really three dimensions in a landscape painting or whether the painter was being intentionally or unintentionally deceptive.

Scientific accounts of origins supplement but do not supplant the purpose of myths. The rise of modern geology and biology has unwittingly done an important service to the proper understanding of creation myths. Widely found fossilized remains and widely accepted evolutionary theories have made it obvious to nearly all educated people that these myths do not describe historical facts. However, people trained in our scientific era often know little about the purpose of fiction or about the limitations of science. They do not know how to examine a text except for answers to the methodological *how* question and the temporal *when* question. Nor do they realize that religious myths were intended to address only the theological *who* question and the teleological *why* question. For example, William Jennings Bryan, the chief hero of the fundamentalists, displayed considerable ignorance of content and form of the book he accepted as "the infallible word of God." He claimed that Genesis declares humans to have come from above a few thousand years ago in contrast to the evolutionist who contends that humans have come from below by a gradual process over a much longer period of time.[8] Actually the Genesis myth-maker avoids such an either/or outlook: humans are there portrayed as a compound of lowly dust and lofty divinity.

The so-called "scientific creationists," and a multitude of other Americans trained in the wooden literalism of a technocratic culture, are poorly educated in literary analysis. They attempt to read the Bible as a scientific textbook, looking for answers to how and when questions with which the biblical writers were not concerned. The controversy that has arisen in regard to human origins has been caused by arrogant religionists who presume that all important questions can be answered by quoting Bible verses and by arrogant scientists who presume that all these questions can be answered by empirical exploration and laboratory analysis.

The goal of all authentic literary investigation is to uncover what was intended by the writers under study. In the following chapters I will look for fresh answers to these questions: What is the relationship between gender and the person who created humans? Why were men and women created? My role in this book is much like an art restorer who flakes off what has been added over the centuries by disciples of the original masters. The painstaking removal of cultural prejudices is worthwhile because of the insights germane to contemporary life that lie beneath.

Chapter 1

Androgyny in Myths

THEOLOGY

Those sharing the Judeo-Christian heritage have generally assumed that the gender of deity is masculine. Embedded in the Western psyche is a figure resembling the bearded Creator painted by Michelangelo on the ceiling of the Sistine Chapel. That Renaissance artist was indebted to Greco-Roman images of Father Zeus/Jupiter. According to one recent survey, most adult Americans think of God as a male and none think of God as a woman.[1] As for children, the typical outlook is articulated in this letter: "Dear God, Are boys better than girls? I know you are one but try to be fair. Sylvia."[2] When a representative sample of Presbyterians were asked what images came to mind when they thought of God, Father was among the most frequent and Mother was among the least.[3] A 1987 poll by the National Opinion Research Center shows that 6 percent more favor thinking of God as father than in 1984.[4]

Gender stereotyping with respect to the divine has doubtlessly been much influenced by the profuse use of masculine imagery in the Bible. Some scholars as well as most common readers discern nothing but masculinity in the biblical conception of God. Northrop Frye, for example, states unequivocally in his discussion of biblical perspectives: "God is male because that rationalizes the ethos of a patriarchal male-dominated society."[5] But a closer examination of biblical theology discloses a significant vestige of feminine imagery from even more ancient texts.

The earliest biblical writers received some of their language from people who lived in Western Asia long before the Hebrew patriarchs. Cuneiform tablets dating back more than four millennia have been excavated in recent years from the Ebla ruin in Syria. El was a prominent masculine god in that ancient city. He consorted with Eloah (or Elah in Aramaic) and produced many sons and daughters that composed the Mesopotamian pantheon. Anath and Astarte were among the female offspring, whereas Baal and Mot were among the male. The parental deities El and Eloah were honored as remote creators in Canaanite religion, but they were believed to be unable to respond effectively to the annual fertility needs of mortals. As gods emeriti, they were similar to Uranus and Gaea of Greek religion.

Out of this early mythology came *'lh*, the root for the name of deity in several Semitic cultures. Well known is Allah (*al-ilah*, the-God) of the Quran. In the Hebrew Bible, El occasionally refers to the deity worshiped by the Israelites. However, there is a definite preference for Elohim, a composite term for deity which may have been developed through merging El with Eloah (*-ah* is a feminine suffix) and adding a plural (*-im*) ending.[6] Walther Eichrodt succinctly explains that the plural Elohim was used "to express the higher unity subsuming the individual gods and combining in one concept the whole pantheon."[7] Thus Elohim designates the essence of individual male and female deities who had been incorporated into a single divine person. Elohim is used in the Bible some 2,500 times to express the unified totality of godness, and thus the term is usually accompanied by a singular verb. Serving as the generic term for deity, Elohim could have either a female or a male reference. Accordingly, the Israelites called goddess Ashtoreth (Astarte) an *elohim* of the Canaanites.[8]

Recognizing the androgynous components of the name Elohim shines much light on the difficult Genesis 1 passage that tells of human creation. There Elohim pronounces, "Let us make humanity in our image, after our likeness." The text then states, "Elohim created humanity male and female in the divine image." The pronouns "us" and "our" appear to be a remnant of an earlier polytheism. Apparently both genders are incorporated in the divine name because the human sexes reflect the image of Elohim. Since this deity is inclusive of the good personal qualities found in both sexes, it would be as faithful to the Genesis affirmation to say God made woman in *her* own image as to say God made man in *his* own image.

Male interpreters of the Bible overlooked the momentous truth pertaining to the feminine and the divine name until feminist publications a century ago. Elizabeth Stanton crowned a lifetime of feminist efforts by gathering scholarly women to assist her with a new interpretation in a book entitled *The Woman's Bible*. On the image of God passage in Genesis 1, Stanton comments:

> It is evident from the language that there was consultation in the Godhead, and that the masculine and feminine elements were equally represented. . . . The masculine and feminine elements, exactly equal and balancing each other, are as essential to the maintenance of the equilibrium of the universe as positive and negative electricity, the centripetal and centrifugal forces, the laws of attraction which bind together all we know of this planet whereon we dwell and of the system in which we revolve.[9]

Stanton attributes the use of masculine pronouns in reference to deity in the Bible to the "paucity of language" with respect to gender. Her outlook may have been stimulated by this observation of her friend Matilda Gage:

> All the evils which have resulted from dignifying one sex and degrading the other may be traced to this central error: a belief in a trinity of masculine God in One, from which the feminine element is wholly eliminated. And yet

in the scriptural account of the simultaneous creation of man and woman, the text plainly recognizes the feminine as well as the masculine element in the Godhead, and declares the equality of the sexes in goodness, wisdom, and power.[10]

The Song of Moses gives another example from the Pentateuch of the way in which both genders point to the nature of the God whom the Israelites worshiped. What has been said in this regard about Elohim can also be said of Yahweh, the covenantal name of the God of Israel. In Deuteronomy 32:6 is one of the few images in the Hebrew Bible of Yahweh as a male progenitor: "Is not he your father, who created you?" However, that same song extols the motherhood as well as the fatherhood of God. In Deuteronomy 32:18 praise is given to "the God who gave you birth." The Hebrew verb here refers to a woman in labor. Apropos here is a comment of James Muilenburg: "Yahweh has no mother goddess at his side; he includes within his nature both husband and wife, both father and mother. The feminine attributes as well as the masculine are absorbed into his holy being."[11] Thus, the Song of Moses says, in effect, that neither maleness nor femaleness should be considered a defining characteristic of God. Parental metaphors are symbols and should not be used to stereotype the divine nature. Even so, paternal and maternal analogies serve to convey that God is the source of existence and the one on whom humans depend for their nurture.

There is a point of comparison between God of Israel and playwright Euripides' depiction of a Greek god. Thomas Rosenmeyer comments on the Bacchae drama:

Dionysus appears to be neither woman nor man; or better, he presents himself as woman-in-man, or man-in-woman, the unlimited personality. . . . In the person of the god strength mingles with softness, majestic terror with coquettish glances. To follow him or to comprehend him we must ourselves give up our precariously controlled, socially desirable sexual limitations.[12]

Dionysus illustrates what anthropologist Justine McCabe writes about a common belief in ancient cultures: "Androgynous deities were the epitome of health, of the sacred, of the reconciliation of the masculine and feminine sides of the human being."[13]

In another division of the Hebrew Bible there are additional insights on the relationship between gender and the divine. Hosea calls Yahweh the husband of Israel while explicitly rejecting the maleness (*ish*) of deity.[14] Isaiah is also bold in word-pictures pertaining to God that cannot be interpreted literally. Using the marital analogy introduced by Hosea, the prophet declares, "Your Creator is your husband." But Isaiah also portrays Yahweh as a suffering and sympathetic woman. Wishing to convey to depressed Jewish exiles that they are not deserted, he proclaims in Yahweh's name, "I will comfort you as a mother comforts her child."[15] Also, in sequential verses Yahweh is described as being "like a mighty man" and "like a woman." As God's spokesperson, Isaiah tells of the pangs attending the rebirth of the people of God: "I will cry out like a woman in labor; I will gasp and pant."[16] Again, to those who felt Godforsaken, the prophet speaks:

> Can a woman forget her baby at the breast,
> Feel no compassion for the child she has borne?
> Even if a mother should forget,
> I will never forget you.[17]

The Hebrew term for compassion comes from the word for womb. Due to modern medicine, suffering in childbirth is now not so intense, but in the biblical culture the parturient experience was regarded as the most graphic way of picturing agonizing but productive suffering. Isaiah thought of God's suffering love as being like the painfulness, tenderness, and joyfulness associated with childbirth.

Isaiah presumed that his lyrical oracles would be taken seriously, but not literally. Frequently, on behalf of God, he asks, "To whom will you liken me?" The implied answer to this rhetorical question is that God is beyond exact comparison. Andromorphic and gynomorphic metaphors are thus intended to convey something about the divine nature, but they are only pointing signs. Isaiah satirized idol-makers who presumed that the transcendent God could be identified with objects of human experience.[18] He shared in a doctrine that an Israelite writer put into a sermon of Moses: "When Yahweh spoke to you out of the fire on Sinai you saw no form. Beware lest you act corruptly by making for yourselves an idol in any form at all — whether male or female. . . . "[19]

Was Isaiah only concerned with eliminating the carving or casting of physical images? The fact that he alternated between male and female images in his theological poetry suggests that his iconoclasm extended to rigid mental as well as material forms. John Calvin, a leader of the Protestant Reformation, so interpreted the Hebrew prophets. He fathomed the psychology of idolatry: "Man's mind, full as it is of pride and boldness, dares to imagine a god according to its own capacity. . . . Man tries to express in his work the sort of God he has inwardly conceived. Therefore the mind begets an idol."[20] Whereas Calvin realized that few Christians are motivated to manufacture and worship graven images, he also realized that the modern disinterest in physical idols should not be equated with faithful allegiance to the Second Commandment. He detected a more insidious way in which hardened images are made inwardly in human minds and then labeled God. Throughout Judeo-Christian history, mental idol factories have produced more patriarchal deities than anything else.

Calvin shares the prophetic iconoclasm when he conceives of God in other than exclusively male terms. His commentary on Isaiah states that maternal images convey better the depth of divine love: "What amazing affection does a mother feel toward her offspring, which she cherishes in her bosom, suckles on her breast, and watches over with tender care, so that she passes sleepless nights, wears herself out by continued anxiety, and forgets herself!" Again, Calvin compares God to "a mother who singularly loves her child though she brought him forth with extreme pain."[21]

Persistent demand for the dominant father image is advocated by those who find the status quo comfortable. Consider, for example, some reasons given for opposing the ordination of women. An Episcopal bishop writes: "The male image about God pertains to the divine initiative in creation. Initiative is, in itself, a male rather than a female attribute."[22] According to another male, "the male priest reflects the creative activity of God the Father."[23] Revealed here is an all too typical adoration of attributes presumed to be exclusively masculine.

In contrast to perennial patriarchal idolatry, the Israelite prophets declare that a deity worthy of worship overwhelms the pictures we sketch in our minds or craft with our hands. Neither man nor woman provides a completely adequate similarity or dissimilarity to the genderless deity.

Some recent research confirms the viewpoint on theological vocabulary expressed here. British scholar Mary Hayter states: "God stands quite outside human sexual differentiation as masculine or feminine. . . . Biblical symbols modulate with amazing versatility, and we abuse them if we try to insist that the grammatical gender of the image is indicative of the essential maleness or femaleness of the referent."[24]

A United Church of Christ study group has elaborated on the way the being worshiped in the religion of Israel transcends gender:

> Yahweh is neither he nor she, not one sex requiring the other to be complete, not asexual and not even an androgynous or "bisexual god" according to some specious theory of a "higher sex," "third sex" or "composite sex." All theories and theologies which impute specific sexuality to God commit the primary and primordial human sin — confusing the Creator with the human creature, which can end only in the confusion of the creature with God, or idolatry.[25]

Some contemporary theologians are attempting to revive the biblical outlook on God. Hans Kung writes: "Today less than ever may the one God be seen merely within a masculine-paternal framework, as an all-too-masculine theology used to present him. The feminine-maternal element in him must also be recognized."[26] Ironically, the pronouns in this quotation may betray that this Catholic priest is devoted to a father-God who has some feminine features. Another highly respected German theologian has, more consistently, pointed to a God beyond patriarchy or matriarchy. Jurgen Moltmann thinks God should be imaged as both a motherly father and a fatherly mother.[27] Such theologizing can better bring out God's care, protection, and closeness.

American theologian Herbert Richardson tells of the impact made on him as a child by a prayer of Mary Baker Eddy. Framed on a wall in his home were these words:

> Father–Mother God
> Loving me
> Guard me while I sleep
> Guide my little feet up to Thee.

Richardson comments:

> I knew that not only was God *both* a Father and a Mother (and therefore like something more than any one thing I experienced around me), but also that my mother and my father — and some mysterious relation between them — was the way God was present in the world. I am convinced that this early experience and teaching concerning the divine androgyny as a norm by which every human being, male or female, is to live has shaped all of my mature theological reflection.[28]

ANTHROPOLOGY

Myths and metaphors about deity are recapitulated in stories of the way men and women originated. Mircea Eliade, the eminent historian of religions, relates theology to anthropology in his extensive writings. "Human androgyny has as its model divine bisexuality," is his dictum.[29] Eliade finds in many ancient cultures stories about an androgyne who was the earliest human ancestor. In the beginning, according to Hinduism, there existed one solitary person who was twice as large as subsequent humans. Being lonely and unhappy, the giant divided "like the half of a split pea." That fission prompted the halves to find one another and become fused in marriage.[30] Zorastrian mythology provides another example: the first human in the earthly paradise was an androgyne out of whom the male Mashye and the female Mashyane separated. The God, Ahura Mazda, warned these "parents of the world" of the evil they would encounter.[31]

The two most famous androgynous myths are found in Plato's *Symposium* and in Genesis. Significant insights are contained in those Greek and Hebrew stories about sexual status and the nature of love. The *Symposium* dialogue contains tributes to love (*eros*) by Athenian men who are participants in a banquet. When comic playwright Aristophanes' turn arises, he spins an androgynous tale. In abridged form, here is his amusing myth:

> Once upon a time human nature was different from what it is now. At first there were three kinds of humans: a double male, a double female, and an androgyne. Each was round, with its back and ribs forming the outside of a sphere. It had four arms, four legs, and double the number of organs. There was one head with two opposite faces on a circular neck. These beings walked upright, but when they wanted to run fast they used their eight limbs to roll over rapidly — like tumblers who perform cart-wheels. Having terrific strength and much arrogance, they tried to climb up to heaven to make war on the gods.

The council of gods debated what should be done to the humans. Extinguishing them with lightning—as they had the titans—was rejected, since this would deprive the gods of worship and sacrifices. Yet they could not allow human insolence to go unrestrained. After much reflection, Zeus had a bright idea. He said: "I think I have found a scheme which can stop the violence of humans by making them weaker. I will bisect each of them and thereby diminish their power." So he sliced humans longitudinally through the middle and told Apollo to turn their faces and genitals toward the surgery and then provide healing. After the original bodies had been cut in two, each half yearned for the half from which it had been served. When they met they entwined their arms around each other and desired to grow together.

So you see how ancient is the mutual love implanted in humans, bringing together the parts of the three original bodies. Love tries to make one out of two in order to heal wounds which humanity suffered. Heterosexual attraction has resulted from splitting the primordial androgyne while homosexual attraction has resulted from splitting the double man or the double female. Some call homosexuals shameless, but they are wrong; boldness and virility makes them welcome the company of their own kind. Boy-lovers avoid marriage and procreation unless compelled by custom. When one half meets the other half, whether boy-lover or anyone else, then the pair are wonderfully overwhelmed by friendship, intimacy, and love. They are the people who form lifelong partnerships.

Thus, human nature was originally a whole, and love is simply the name for the desire and pursuit of the whole. If lovers were perfectly fulfilled, and each one returned to their primeval nature and had their original true love, then humankind would be happy. Therefore, if we would praise the one who has given us this benefit, we must praise Eros. By bringing us back in this life to our own nature, that god is our greatest benefactor. Those who are devoted to Eros will be restored to their original state, which will provide them with healing and happiness.32

When Plato wrote his dialogues, he was probably unaware that earlier in the same millennium an Israelite recorded an androgynous myth. The composer is called the Yahwist by scholars, because Yahweh is the preferred name for deity. In the abridged form, the Yahwist's story follows:

Elohim Yahweh formed the human from the humus [the Hebrew pun is *adam* from *adamah*]. On receiving the breath of life, the human became a living being. Then Yahweh planted a park in Eden and placed the human there to care for it.

Yahweh said, "It is not good for the human to live alone; I will make a suitable partner." So out of the ground Yahweh formed every animal; but not one of them proved to be a peer. Then Yahweh caused the human to fall into a hypnotic trance in order to remove a part of the body. Closing up the flesh, Yahweh fashioned the part into a woman. When she was brought to the man, he exclaimed: "This one at last is bone of my bones and flesh of my flesh! She shall be called *gyne* because she was taken from *andros* [using the translations of the Greek Septuagint, which accurately denotes the gender distinction but does not convey the Hebrew pun, *ishah* from *ish*]."

That is why an *andros* leaves his father and his mother and clings to his *gyne*, so that the two become one flesh. Now they were both naked, the husband and his wife, but they were unashamed.33

The Eden narrative, like Aristophanes' speech, is a delightful fantasy. Although neither was intended to be interpreted as matter-of-fact hominid history, both convey profound psychological and theological meaning. There are both similarities and differences in the content of the two stories.

A theme pervading both myths is that the sexes share a fundamental equality. The deity in each makes no superiority-inferiority ranking of the pristine human's parts which become sexually separated.

Christian interpreters have occasionally detected this theme of male-female parity repeated in the Bible. Stanton perceptively related her comprehension of normative biblical anthropology to nineteenth-century Christianity:

> The Old Testament, "in the beginning," proclaims the simultaneous creation of man and woman, the eternity and equality of sex. . . . Paul, in speaking of equality as the very soul and essence of Christianity, said, "There is neither Jew nor Greek, there is neither bond nor free, there is neither male nor female; for ye are all one in Christ Jesus." With this recognition of the feminine element in the Godhead in the Old Testament, and this declaration of the equality of the sexes in the New, we may well wonder at the contemptible status woman occupies in the Christian Church of today.[34]

Eliade also quotes the apostle's affirmation pertaining to ideal personhood and comments: "This is the unity of primal creation, before the making of Eve, when 'man' was neither male nor female." Eliade notes that Paul "counted androgyny as one of the characteristics of spiritual perfection."[35]

Jesus is represented in early Christianity as having an androgynous outlook similar to that of Paul. When asked about when God's reign would come, Jesus replied: "When the two become one . . . and the male with the female neither male nor female." In that second-century sermon, this interpretation is given Jesus' reply: "When a Christian man sees a Christian woman he should not think of her as female, nor she of him as male."[36]

Another idea contained in the Greek and Hebrew myths under consideration is that sex is a sectioning. The term *sex* comes from the Latin verb *secare*, to cut, and Aristophanes' speech is probably the etymological source of the metaphor. The similarity of the myths is more apparent if a key word of the Hebrew account is examined. *Tsela* is presumed in translations to mean "rib" even though the Hebrew does not suggest a specific part of the body. Apart from the Eden story the other biblical uses of *tsela* have a nonanatomical reference, and usually mean "side." In Exodus 26:20, for example, it refers to "the *side* of the tabernacle." The assumption that a rib was extracted is due to a guess by the Greek translators. It seems that the original story told of the removal of one side of a composite human.

Medieval Judaism was aware that Genesis tells of the dividing of a primeval androgyne. The Talmud conceives of the human prior to severance as being Janus-like, having a face looking either way.[37] Rabbi Samuel ben Nahman explained that the human had "a double face which was then severed in two."[38] When God split the sleeping androgyne with an axe, woman became the right side and man the left side.[39]

The androgynous myths picture not only an original wholeness and a sexual separation, but also a voluntary splicing. The main purpose of sexual intercourse among humans is lovemaking, not baby-making. An individual searches for one who is his or her complement and then reunites the self by means of mutual embracing. Both myths express in their own way the powerful compulsion that lovers experience to overcome their sense of fragmentation. Aristophanes tells of the hemispheres wanting to become a total sphere and of a joyful pair bonding when this purpose is accomplished. In order to heighten this same point, the Hebrew story contrasts *adam*'s futile search for companionship with other animal species. The human feels too different from the fauna to find in that realm partnership and personal fulfillment.

Catholic interpreter George Tavard recognizes that *ha-adam* has no sexual connotation in Genesis 2 and sees significance in the new Hebrew names. He writes: "From his companionship with woman, man obtains his name of glory,

that which expresses his condition as a being-in-relationship.
... The sex-name of man is his other name, *Ish*, by which he relates to woman, *Ishah*."[40]

The Genesis myth of mutual sexual dependence became a
central teaching of the Christian gospel. On the Eden story of
symbiosis, Jesus commented: "What then God has joined
together, let no one separate."[41] Jesus saw divine activity in
synthesis as well as in the initial creation and in the sexual
separation. The total human then is not a singular biped, but a
"two in one flesh" being. Accordingly, G. K. Chesterton has
called marriage in the biblical tradition "the great four-footed
thing, the quadruped of the home."[42]

There are also some distinctive differences between these
Greek and Hebrew myths. Aristophanes claims the bisection
of the whole human was due to the Olympian pantheon feeling threatened by the power of mortals. However, the deities
craved the homage rendered by humans, so they did not want
to kill them. The huge beings are thus cut to suppress their
rebel impulse to usurp the gods' control over the world. Zeus
also warns that he might slice hubristic humans, again, leaving
one-legged persons.

In the Eden story, by contrast, the single God has no anxiety
over being bested by humans, so no cruel action is needed for
self-protection. After the divine Potter inspires a mud figure
and thus makes an androgyne — the primary creative act — a differentiation is made between the male and the female — a
secondary act — in order to relieve human solitariness.
Sexuality becomes simultaneous for both when surgery is performed. Loneliness is overcome when two from opposite sexes
find companionship they deem fitting and become reunited.

The most striking difference between these anthropological
myths is in the types of gender bonding approved in the two ancient cultures. Homosexual as well as heterosexual passion is endorsed by Aristophanes, although he admits that some fellow
Greeks find homosexuality revolting. The Yahwist myth
celebrates heterosexual monogamy and, by implication, disap-

proves of homosexual coupling. The story culminates with clutching lovers—who, in gender-related Anglicized Greek, might be called Andy and Cora. The infusion of the opposite sex affords the spouses a fuller self-identification and a guiltless satisfaction.

Social scientists are now finding that androgyny myths reflect much of what they are now learning about the oneness of human nature. Studies by anthropologists and psychologists indicate that the terms "feminine" and "masculine" are used improperly in reference to inborn psychological traits and properly in reference to biological differences—genital organs and their functions, voice depth, body hair, and physique. Only one of the 23 pairs of chromosomes of the fertilized ovum is different as to sex, and this appropriately reflects the ratio of natural differences to similarities.

Margaret Mead, as a result of a pioneering field study in New Guinea, became persuaded that the "natural sex temperament" that she went out to discover was a fiction. In the Mundugumor tribe, women were fiercely combative and disliked child care responsibilities. By contrast, the Arapesh were nurturing and mild people and this was expressed by both sexes being entertained by dolls and being alarmed by crying babies. The Tchambuli tribe were different from both in that their women aggressively organized the community and took the initiative in sex, whereas their men were impractical and emotionally dependent. Mead concluded that "many, if not all, of the personality traits which we have called masculine or feminine are as lightly linked to sex as are the clothing, the manners, and the form of head-dress that a society at a given period assigns to either sex."[43]

Anthropologists have found many other instances of socialization's heavy impact in particular cultures on the prevailing patterns of traits appropriate to males and females. Some societies hold stereotypes that are similar to those of Western civilization, but many hold quite different ones. If our women tend to be more tenderhearted and our men more hardheaded this is best understood as the result of early nurture, not innate nature.

A number of investigations of sex-typing have disclosed the subtle ways by which parents mold stereotypical, sex-appropriate behavior during the first few years of their children's lives.[44] A study of genetically identical twin males by John Money and Anke Ehrhardt shows conclusively the malleability of male and female temperaments. The penis of one of the infants was accidentally burned off by electrocautery when circumcision was intended. Consequently the parents decided to raise the child as a girl. Wearing dresses and long hair, "she" was trained to act like a little lady. She grew up with what our society would call traditional femininity while her twin brother acquired what we would call masculinity.[45] This proves that what a culture calls masculine and feminine traits are due more to acculturation then to genes, hormones, or brain structures.

Psychologist Sandra Bem has developed a sex role inventory which lists 60 personality characteristics for the purpose of measuring how masculine, feminine, or androgynous a person is. Stereotypical feminine qualities on her scale include affectionate, sensitive, understanding, loyal, and soft-spoken. Masculine qualities include self-reliant, athletic, forceful, analytical, and competitive. The androgynous individual is "both independent and tender, assertive and yielding." Bem's research indicates that those identified as androgynous tend to surpass stereotypical masculine or feminine persons in creativity and intelligence.[46]

After reviewing contemporary gender research Deborah Belle observes:

Despite widespread belief to the contrary, virtually all studies of sex differences in cognitive skills, temperament, and social behavior as elicited in laboratory settings show striking similarity between men and women. . . . The repeated finding of minimal or no sex differences across a wide variety of skills, styles, and behaviors argues against the notion that the two sexes differ sharply in their intrinsic capacities for cognitive and social behavior.[47]

Mythmakers who assessed personality in the Hebrew and Greek cultures associated full human life with a blending of characteristics from both genders. The ancient attention to androgyny has been revived during the past generation by social scientists who are devoted to finding developmental patterns that do not restrict human maturity. All have found that androgyny, not anatomy, is destiny.

Chapter 2

A Bone of Contention

Due to the preeminence of European translations of the adamic creation story, no portion of the human skeleton has generated more theological consideration than the ribs. That part of the anatomy was especially intriguing because of the biblical literalists' belief that all sons of Adam inherit one less rib than the daughters of Eve.

The clash between biology and literalism began with Andreas Vesalius who boldly stated in 1543 that the rib cages of both sexes contain the same number of bones. The founder of modern anatomy wrote: "The ribs are twelve in number on each side in man and woman. . . . The popular belief that man is lacking a rib on one side and that woman has one more rib than man is clearly ridiculous, even though Moses, in the second chapter of Genesis, said that Eve was created by God from one of Adam's ribs."[1] Vesalius was heavily criticized for stating an easily verifiable empirical fact. Along with other Gentiles, he wrongly assumed that a rib bone was explicitly referred to in the original Hebrew.

Now that the literal meaning of the Genesis creation story is generally rejected among educated people, the rib operation is popularly afforded little more than facetious comments. Ribald males may pun that woman is unfortunately not abreast of man, but only a side issue. Another offensive "joke" suggests that woman was taken from man's lower ribs, midway between his heart and his wallet, to symbolize that she was destined to control both.

In what follows, such ribbing will be discounted in an attempt to look seriously at treatments of the rib motif in the Judeo-Christian tradition. What do the varied uses of that motif reveal about perceptions of woman's proper place? There are no explicit references to Adam's rib in the biblical era apart from its single mention in Genesis, so our survey will be confined to the postbiblical era. The interpretations that have emerged over the past two millennia can be grouped into these three categories: androcentric, gynocentric, and egalitarian.

THE CROOKED RIB

Considering the historical dominance by males, it is not surprising that the androcentric category contains the largest number of contributions. In Judaism, comments about Adam's rib were frequently uncomplimentary to women. One sermon extols what was presumed to be woman's noblest virtue, while denouncing her alleged vices. God deliberated, so we are told, from which part of man to create woman.

> I will not create her from the head for she may carry herself haughtily; nor from the eye for she may be too inquisitive; nor from the ear for she may be an eavesdropper; nor from the mouth for she may be too talkative; nor from the heart for she may be too jealous; nor from the hand for she may be too acquisitive; nor from the foot for she may be a gadabout. I will create her from a hidden part of the body that she may be modest; even when man stands naked, his rib is covered.[2]

This midrash on Genesis goes on to say that God's careful planning miscarried, for woman is conceited, curious, a gossip, a chatterbox, envious, grasping, and a gadabout.

Some Rabbinic Jews associated bone properties with characteristics believed to be feminine:

Why is it that only woman needs perfume? Man was created from earth which does not putrefy but Eve was created from a bone. If you leave meat unsprinkled with spices it soon reeks.

And why has a woman a penetrating voice, but not a man? If you fill a pot with meat it does not make any sound, but when you put a bone into it, the sound spreads immediately.

And why is a man easily appeased, but not a woman? Man was created from a clod of earth and when you pour a drop of water on it, it immediately absorbs it, but Eve was created from a bone which remains hard even after being submerged for days.[3]

Those Jewish viewpoints are similar to the outlook of Muhammad, a fellow Semite who honored the stories of the Bible. According to Muslim tradition, he said: "Admonish your wives with kindness, for woman was created from a rib. You will break her if you try to straighten her out, so use her with her crookedness."[4]

Christian scholars also attempted to explain why it was fitting for God to create woman from a rib. Augustine associated a rib more with flesh than with bone: "Flesh stands for woman, because she was made out of a rib. . . . Flesh thus stands for the wife, as sometimes also spirit for the husband. Why? Because the latter rules, the former is ruled; the latter should govern, the former serve."[5]

Thomas Aquinas restated an idea he received from Augustine in this comment about woman: "She was not fitted to help man except in generation, because another man would have proved a more effective help in anything else."[6] Aquinas thought woman was made for "social union," that is, for procreative coupling:

It was right for the woman to be made from a rib of man . . . to signify the social union of man and woman; for the woman should not use authority over man, and so she was not made from his head; nor was it right for her to be subject to man's contempt as his slave, and so she was not made from his feet.[7]

Among Aquinas's many borrowings from Aristotle was the judgment that "the female is a mutilated male."[8] However, that Dominican monk was hesitant to accept Aristotle's description as completely true, for he found no defect in woman's reproductive equipment.[9] For Aquinas, woman was essentially a womb-man.

Two centuries later two other Dominicans combined the views of Aristotle and Muhammad. In a manual devoted to describing the nature of witches, Heinrich Kramer and James Sprenger wrote: "There was a defect in the formation of the first woman, since she was formed from a bent rib, that is, a rib of the breast, which is bent as it were in a contrary direction to a man. And since through this defect she is an imperfect animal, she always deceives."[10]

Joseph Swetnam carried the crooked rib theme into Elizabethan England when he wrote:

A woman was made to be a helper, and so they are indeed: for she helpeth to spend and consume that which man painefully getteth. . . . They were made of the ribbe of a man, and that their froward nature sheweth; for a ribbe is a crooked thing, good for nothing else, and women are crooked by nature, for small occasion will cause them to be angry.[11]

Swetnam's treatment of woman was popular, for his book entitled *The Araignment of Lewde, Idle, Froward, and Unconstant Women* went through 14 editions over several centuries.

Also widely read and translated in the seventeenth century was *Religio Medici* by English physician Thomas Browne. This was his gender outlook: "The whole world was made for man, but the twelfth part of man for woman: man is the whole world, and the breath of God; woman the rib and crooked piece of man." Armed with this theological anthropology, he helped to convict women of witchcraft.

In the same era, an even more scurrilous attack on woman was given wide circulation in Europe. It was probably stimulated by a comment in the Talmud that the Hebrew word *tsela* in Genesis 2:22 refers to a bone no longer found in man. The rabbis were honestly puzzled by the term because, as we have seen, it was used in Hebrew to refer to a part of a body only in the story of woman's creation. Only after being translated into Greek did *tsela*, Hebrew for "side," come to mean specifically "rib."

Some rabbis speculated that *tsela* was the tail Adam once possessed,[12] and this resulted in the spinning of a denigrating story about how a dog frustrated the divine plan for creating woman. It seems that while God was washing up after performing surgery on Adam, a dog stole and devoured the part that had been removed. God then resorted to cutting off the dog's tail and forming woman from it. This method of creation is used to explain certain alleged doglike characteristics of woman. Both creatures were said to wag their hind quarters or bark at their masters when they want attention. This story was disseminated around 1550 in England by Edward Gosynill's *Schole House of Women*, and in Germany by a long poem of Hans Sachs, an ardent Lutheran.[13]

Irish poet Thomas Moore called the story of the rib a "fib." In coarse humor that demeans both Eve and Adam, he elaborates on the tail tale:

> The Old Adam was fashioned, the first of his kind,
> With a tail like a monkey, full yard and a span
> And then nature cut off his appendage behind,
> Why, then woman was made of the tail of the
>   man. . . .
> Every husband remembers the original plan
> And knowing his wife is no more than his tail
> Why, he leaves her behind him as much as he can.[14]

Antifeminist sentiment, alleged to be Bible based, is found in an anonymous drama named *The Taming of a Shrew*. The play interested Shakespeare, so he adapted it and retained the title. The heroine works over a perverse etymological pun:

> A rib was taken, of which the Lord did make
> The woe of man, so termed by Adam then
> "Wo-man," for that by her came sin to us;
> And for her sin was Adam doomed to die.
> As Sarah to her husband, so should we
> Obey them, love them, keep, and nourish them.
> If they by any means do want our help,
> Lay our hands under their feet to tread.[15]

Seventeenth-century interpretations of Adam's rib were somewhat more charitable. Jesuit Francis de Sales wrote:

Woman was taken from that side of the first man which was nearest his heart, to the end that she might be loved by him cordially and tenderly. . . . God . . . was pleased to ordain that the woman should depend upon the man, being bone of his bone and flesh of his flesh, and that she should be made of a rib taken from under his arm, to show that she ought to be under the hand and guidance of her husband.[16]

Puritan John Milton also associated the rib cage with the coronary organ which it surrounds. Adam, in *Paradise Lost*, speaks endearingly of the way his "other half" was formed: "Out of my side to thee, neerest my heart."[17] Adam expresses an ambivalence toward Eve, for she is a lovely creature but an imperfect expression of the divine image in man. He laments that the one he has been given to rule is "a Rib crooked by nature":

> O why did God,
> Creator wise, that peopl'd highest Heav'n
> With Spirits Masculine, create at last
> This noveltie on Earth, this fair defect
> Of Nature, and not fill the World at once
> With Men as Angels without Feminine,
> Or find some other way to generate Mankind?[18]

In a tract advocating the right of divorce, Milton viewed Adam's rib as having the potential to become a large, painful thorn when it is returned to its original place in marriage. Milton wrote in reference to Adam: "If God took a rib out of his inside, to form of it a double good to him, he would far sooner dis-joyn it from his outside, to prevent a treble mischief to him . . . then nail it into his body again, to stick for ever there a thorn in his heart."[19] Paul's "thorn in the flesh" imagery is probably alluded to here. Medieval celibates had presumed that the apostle was referring to pain brought by the opposite sex.

Richard Whitlock, an English contemporary of Milton, considered a jawbone to be more apt than a thorn for comparison with the rib. He vituperated: "I am confident a practicing Rib shall kill more then the Jaw-bone of an Asse; and a quacking Dalilah, then a valiant Sampson."[20] But Lord Byron appropriated Milton's figure, and has Don Juan remark that "a rib's a thorn in a wed gallant's side."[21]

In recent times the androcentric interpretation of Adam's rib has continued unabated. Several representative treatments from the past century will be cited. Elizabeth Stanton, a leading suffragette, believed the story of Adam's rib was intended to teach "that woman was made after man, of man, and for man, an inferior being, subject to man."[22] According to James Frazer, the ancient mythmaker had a "deep contempt for woman": "The lateness of her creation, and the irregular and undignified manner of it—made out of a piece of her Lord and master, after all the lower animals had been created in a regular and decent manner — sufficiently mark the low opinion he held of her nature."[23]

Theologian Rosemary Ruether writes: "The story of the creation of a woman from the rib of the original man to be his helpmeet clearly located 'woman's place' as derivative and auxiliary."[24] Contemporary feminists Simone de Beauvoir, Paula Stern, and Kate Millett have also accepted the traditional male chauvinist interpretation. They think the rib story was intended to portray woman as a divine afterthought, fashioned from an insignificant portion of the masculine frame.[25]

THE PRIME RIB

The foregoing androcentric interpretations of the contentious bone can be partly offset by sexism of an opposite kind. Since most writings in history have been composed by males, it is understandable that philogynistic interpretations of Adam's rib are more scarce than the misogynistic ones.

The postbiblical Jewish tradition can probably be given the credit for the first gynocentric interpretation. The Talmud contains this tale:

> A Gentile ruler said to Rabbi Gamaliel, "Your God is a thief, because he stole one of Adam's ribs." Thereupon the rabbi's daughter said to her father, "Leave him to me; I will answer him." Turning to the ruler she exclaimed, "Thieves broke into our house and stole a silver vessel, leaving a gold one in its place!" The ruler laughed and said, "I wish I could have burglars like that every day." "Well," she retorted, "that is what our God did: he took a mere rib from the first man but in exchange he gave him a wife."[26]

If the analogy between wife and gold is pressed, then this bit of Jewish lore treats woman as husband-owned property and it would better be assigned an androcentric classification. But in Judaism women were not valued as precious because of chattel status.

During the age of chivalry women were occasionally rhapsodized. Humbert de Romans, a thirteenth-century master general of the Dominican friars, asserted: "God gave women many prerogatives, not only over other living things but even over man himself. . . . In the world of nature she excelled man by her origin, for . . . man he formed of the slime, but woman of man's rib."[27]

John Dryden, a seventeenth-century poet, interpreted the rib story to mean that the male was what was left after the best was extracted. A lady boasts:

> Our sex, you know, was after yours designed:
> The last perfection of the Maker's mind.
> Heaven drew out all the gold for us
> And left our dross behind.[28]

Fellow Englishman William Austin, during the same century, affirmed that woman was made from a more refined substance than the "slyme" from which man was made. He believed that there was an ascending sequence in the creation: from inorganic, to plant, to animal, to human. Then, within the human species, the female follows the male. Austin asserts: "Every worke being still more perfect, . . . he rested as having finished all in her, beyond whose perfection no creature more could be added, created, or imagined."[29] Scotsman Robert Burns gave poetic expression to the view that woman was Mother Nature's improved copy of humanity:

> Auld Nature swears the lovely dears
> Her noblest work she classes, O:
> Her 'prentice han' she tried on man,
> And then she made the lasses, O![30]

In the early eighteenth century, Alexander Pope muses on the loneliness of his earliest ancestor:

Our grandsire, Adam, ere of Eve possess'd,
Alone, and ev'n in Paradise, unblest
With mournful looks the blissful scenes survey'd
And wander'd in the solitary shade.
The Maker saw, took pity, and bestow'd
Woman, the last, the best reserv'd by God.[31]

The advent of social Darwinism made this maxim popular: later development implies higher quality. A century ago Lillie Blake argued: "It cannot be maintained that woman was inferior to man even if . . . she was created after him, without at once admitting that man is inferior to the creeping things because he was created after them." According to Blake, the rib episode treats woman as "the last and crowning glory of the whole."[32]

More recently, biblical scholar Phyllis Trible has argued that the Eden story shows that woman, although last in time, is first in quality:

She is the culmination. . . . To call woman "Adam's rib" is to misread the text which states carefully and clearly that the extracted bone required divine labor to become female, a datum scarcely designed to bolster the male ego. . . . By contrast he is formed from dirt; his life hangs by a breath which he does not control; and he himself remains silent and passive while the Deity plans and interprets his existence. . . . Throughout the myth she is the more intelligent one, the more aggressive one, and the one with greater sensibilities.[33]

Trible reinforces the outlook of biblical theologian Samuel Terrien: "The order of creation goes from the imperfect to the perfect. Woman constitutes the crowning of creation. . . . While the woman exercises critical judgment in her dialogue with the serpent, the man does not even argue with her. . . . She is a real person. Man is a brute."[34]

George Tavard anchors his view on woman's status in the

Septuagint, which tells of Yahweh "building" the rib into woman (*ishah*). He writes:

There is only one creation, that of Adam. The next step does not come as a second process of creation, but as a step within the total process or as a further development. . . . *Ishah* proceeds from inside of Adam, where she was already present as that to which mankind was destined, as the development that would bring it to perfection, as the identity with a difference which makes society-building possible. "This is bone of my bone and flesh of my flesh." Mankind recognizes itself in *Ishah*. . . . In this revelation Adam perceives clearly what his confrontation with the animals had only weakly hinted at, his personality. Adam becomes a person, aware of himself, reaching consciousness as mankind at the unveiling of woman. For woman also is mankind. She is no other than Adam; but she is Adam as bringing to perfection what had first been imperfect. She is mankind as fully aware of its status, as the goal and perfection of man.[35]

Some feminists speculate that the Genesis account of Adam's rib is a patriarchal transvaluation of a more archaic story. Elizabeth Davis claims that some Hebrew male so resented the humiliation of being born of woman that he recast a matriarchal myth about "the Great Goddess, Eve." She claims: "The whole intention of the distortion manifested in the Hebrew tale of Adam and Eve is twofold: first, to deny the tradition of a female creator; and second, to deny the original supremacy of the female sex."[36] Theologian Mary Daly agrees with Davis's contention that the Genesis story of woman's creation is a ludicrous falsification, affirming as it does "that Eve was born from Adam, the first among history's unmarried pregnant males who courageously chose childbirth under sedation rather than abortion, consequently obtaining a child-bride."[37] Daly states that scientific truth is inverted in Aristotle's belief that female embryos are defects in nature's plan to produce all

males. The male, she asserts, should be thought of as a mis-
begotten female because he is produced by a Y chromosome —
which is an incomplete X chromosome.[38]

THE EQUAL PARTNER

Over against the androcentric and gynocentric interpretations, we note the egalitarian interpretation which understands
the rib passage of Genesis to teach that both man and woman
share in the same nature and ought to be accorded the same
dignity.

In 1836, Angelina Grimke, the civil rights pioneer, evaluated
the status of woman in Genesis 2 in this way: "A companion
and equal, not one hair's breadth beneath him in the majesty
and glory of her moral being; not placed under his authority as
a subject, but by his side, on the same platform of human rights,
under the government of God only."[39]

Grimke may have been influenced by a hymn of Charles
Wesley. He modified a medieval interpretation, and making it
explicitly egalitarian:

> Not from his head was woman took,
> As made her husband to o'er-look,
> Not from his feet, as one design'd
> The footstool of the stronger kind;
> But fashion'd for himself, a bride,
> An equal, taken from his side.[40]

This interpretation of the rib passage in Genesis has considerable textual evidence in its favor. Yahweh's experiments
in providing companionship show the inferiority of animals to
the human, not the inferiority of female to male. After the
human discovers the unsuitability of beasts and birds as peers,
a female from the same species is created. Maleness is then discovered in responding to the female. Woman is more than a rib
belonging to her husband, even as *adam* is more than mud

belonging to the earth. God directly created *adam* from the passive earth and woman from the dormant *adam*. Modern interpreters have commonly endorsed an egalitarian interpretation of the Priestly account of male/female creation in Genesis 1, but have assumed that the Priestly editor followed this by a story with an altogether different view of gender status. For example, psychoanalyst Theodor Reik claims that the Eden story is "in contradiction to the first account" where male and female are produced simultaneously and in God's own image. Reik views the Yahwist creation account in Genesis 2 in this sequential manner: initially a male human is formed, then animals, and then a female human.[41] Literary historian Katharine Rogers calls the Eden story "unquestionably misogynist" and treats it as a "contrasting version" to one set down in the previous chapter.[42]

In contrast to these positions some biblical scholars maintain that both the Yahwist story of creation in Genesis 2 and the Priestly account of creation in Genesis 1 have the same view of humankind. Phyllis Bird states: "While the two creation accounts of Genesis differ markedly in language, style, date and traditions employed, their basic statements about woman are essentially the same: woman is, along with man, the direct and intentional creation of God and the crown of his creation."[43] Another exegete, Mary Hayter, offers a similar interpretation:

In Genesis 1 the creation of man and woman is recorded as God's last act in the creative sequence — but there is no implication that this renders mankind secondary and subordinate to all the other living creatures. In Genesis 2, woman is said to have been created after the animals — but there is no hint that she is thereby inferior to them. ... The Yahwist and the Priestly writer both reveal man and woman to share identical humanness, and equal dignity and a common task.[44]

It is implausible that the Priestly writer, who is also the

Genesis editor, would follow his account of gender equality in Genesis 1 with an antifeminist story. The much later two verses on human creation in Genesis 1 should be viewed as a condensed and less anthropomorphic way of asserting the basic teaching of Genesis 2 about both human genders being fashioned by the Creator.

Genesis 1:27 declares that "God created *ha-adam* in his own image" and makes explicit that both male and female belong to this genus. Both components of *adam* are commanded to share the responsibility for populating the earth and taming nature. The husband is not given dominion over his wife, but the spouses are mutually elevated to lordship over creation under the lordship of the Creator. To borrow an exquisite New Testament phrase, they are made to be "cosharers in the grace of life."[45]

Some translations of the original Hebrew make it wrongly appear as though woman is created to perform a subservient sex role. But God formed other creatures, according to the story, so that the human could associate with a fitting companion. In Genesis 2:20 *ezer* is joined by *neged*, to refer to a similar counterpart. Although *ezer neged* has commonly been translated "helpmate" or "fit helper," a better translation would be "a suitable partner." In contemporary parlance a helper refers to a person in a menial position who does unskilled work. However, an examination of the 20 other biblical usages of *ezer* displays that it never connotes someone in a servile role. *Ezer* often refers to a superior person and is frequently associated with divine assistance. For example, a psalmist proclaims, "Happy is he whose helper (*ezer*) is the God of Jacob."[46]

The Hebrew word *adam* has posed a problem for interpreters because, like the English word "man," it can refer either to the human species or to an adult male human. The use of the definite article *ha* explicitly indicates when *adam* is not a personal name. *Adam* is not a proper name in Genesis 2, so translations that render it "Adam" fail to convey its primary meaning.[47] (The New English Bible and the Jerusalem Bible correctly avoid the use of the proper name "Adam" in the creation story. If *ha-adam* refers to man as male then, according to Genesis 3:24, Eve was not cast out of Eden.) At the beginning of the story *ha-adam* is an androgyne containing both sexes. Genesis 2:7 can be translated: "God Yahweh formed wo/man (*ha-adam*) from the soil of mother earth (*adamah*, feminine), breathed into the creature's nostrils, and s/he began to live." This inspirited earthling is put in the Garden of Eden to cultivate it and enjoy it. Yahweh forms other animals and *ha-adam* names them, but they are unable to provide the peer companionship *ha-adam* needs for the good life. To cure this deficiency, a section is performed on the sleeping androgyne and sexual division results. Even as soil was made into the proto-human, so the latter was made into female and male. The diagram that follows expresses the theological anthropology of the Yahwist story:

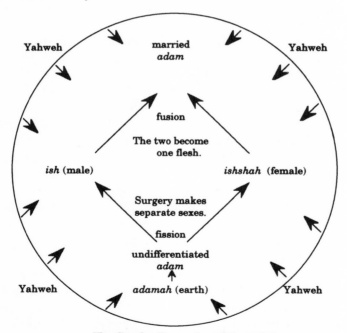

The Gender Dynamics of Genesis 2

Looking back on Eve's three faces — androcentric, gynocentric, egalitarian — it can be seen that she and her daughters have usually been regarded as inferior beings vis-à-vis Adam and his sons. Judging by the literary history of the rib motif, woman has occasionally been regarded as the superior sex. But relatively little attention has been given to a view that avoids both extremes.

Viewpoints on astronomy provide an instructive parallel to sex role outlooks. Through most of human history a geocentric view of the universe was accepted without question. Then Copernicus defended a heliocentric view which had been held many centuries earlier by some Pythagoreans. There are some today who assume that Copernicus was correct in his substitution of the Sun for the Earth as the hub of the universe. Yet Newton showed that neither viewpoint is correct since there is no cosmic center. Rather, there are galaxies galore and each body within the vast universe exerts a mutual gravitational attraction on every other body.

Likewise, in reacting against the traditional androcentric view of humanity, some have endorsed the opposite gynocentric view. A few held this view in an earlier era and, with the swinging of the values pendulum away from patriarchy, more are championing it today. Both views are as myopic as the views of those who have dogmatically declared that our Sun or our planet is at the center of the world. Neither male nor female, neither Sun nor Earth, have ultimate primacy. There is a mutuality between the sexes that the nameless "Newton" of anthropological myths discerned several millennia ago. The myth was preserved at the beginning of the Hebrew Bible and has probably had more circulation than any story ever told.

Due to the pervasive concept of evolutionary progress in our culture, it is often glibly assumed that history has been moving like an arrow away from repression based on gender. However, this rib motif survey shows that the nadir of feminism was during the Renaissance era. It was then that many were obsessed with persecuting alleged witches whose criminal behavior was allegedly caused by their crooked ribs. Contrary to historical progressivism, an egalitarian high point was when the Genesis creation myths were composed and accepted as revelatory. Contained there is the story of a lonely wo/man who finds no full companionship with other animals. It was only after the momentous sexual fission surgery and the accompanying creation that the residual male exclaims, "This one at last is bone of my bone!" As he responds to the woman he understands his own sexuality. Moreover, contrary to patriarchal mores, the *male* leaves his parents in order to "cleave" to his wife.

The myths of one era often contribute to the establishment of social practices at a later time. It is highly significant that Jesus was one of the first Jews to state overtly that he regarded the Genesis 2 story to be normative. He criticized the androcentric law which made divorce the exclusive prerogative of Jewish men, often on trivial grounds. He endorsed the ideal of Gen. 2:24 which states that "the two shall become one embodiment."[48] His philogynous outlook on women was probably partly due to the influence of that Genesis myth. Hopefully, others who are emancipated from warped interpretations of the rib symbol may find in it a divine encouragement for treating each sex as a hemisphere of a psychologically androgynous complete sphere.

Chapter 3

Eve and Pandora

The Hebrew myth of Eve and the Greek myth of Pandora have had profound impact on Western civilization because they allegedly reveal woman's true nature. Scholarly studies as well as popular treatments have generally presumed that both myths aim at alerting men to feminine evil.[1] Theologian J. E. Bruno holds that the myths are two versions of the same story of the first woman.[2] Agreeing with this assessment, classicist Walter Headlam asserts that both myths portray woman as a divine "afterthought" and, in Hesiod's words, "a curse and a bane."[3] According to Frederick Teggart, the pattern of both myths is the same: "First, a state of bliss; second, the mischievous activity of the woman; third, a description of evils. Consequently, it might reasonably be inferred that Hesiod, the Greek who wrote of Pandora, used a variant of a narrative that was also utilized in the story of the Garden of Eden."[4]

Contrary to the prevailing opinion, a close examination of Eve and Pandora in their original text shows them to be quite dissimilar. Our lack of awareness of this difference has been due to interpreters throughout Western civilization who have unwittingly attempted to combine these two myths. In what follows, the earliest written expressions of the independent myths will be examined. Then the way in which Eve has been transformed to resemble Pandora will be traced.

THE HEBREW EVE

The name Eve is not introduced to designate the first woman until the end of the Garden of Eden story. Due to translation and conceptual difficulties, few readers understand that there is no gender differentiation for much of the story. At the beginning, the divine Potter shapes clay and animates the human (*ha-adam*) by blowing breath into its nostrils. The human is provided a garden to till as well as to enjoy and is given the freedom to eat fruit from all trees but one. Realizing that solitary life and work is less than ideal, Yahweh forms other animal species for human companionship. However, satisfaction does not arrive until a second divine experiment is completed. Simultaneously the male (*ish*) and the female (*ishshah*) are created from *ha-adam*. Each sex then seeks the missing part of the divided body. Soon the naked male and female rejoin and "become one flesh."

In the subsequent episode the primeval pair engage in conversation with one another and with others. To assist in identifying the speakers, the husband is once given the proper name Adam (*adam* without the definite article *ha*) and the wife is once called Eve. The serpent initiates the conversation by subtly suggesting that the divine command was a prohibition of all fruit. Eve responds by relating — presumably from knowledge obtained when she was part of the collection human — that the prohibition was limited to one tree. The serpent then persuades Eve that divine wisdom rather than human death will result from eating the forbidden fruit. Regarding the off-limits tree, this is stated: "She took of its fruit and ate; and she gave some to her husband who was with her, and he ate." The jointly disobedient couple then have a misplaced shame over their appearance. Both attempt to transfer responsibility to others and both are punished.

This re-examination of the adamic myth discloses that its composer did not express the male bias that has been characteristic of most subsequent translators and interpreters. To cite one example, they have usually not conveyed that Adam was with Eve at the scene of the crime. The Revised Standard Version, the New English Bible, and Today's English Version are among those following the Latin Vulgate's error of not stating that Adam was with Eve in the encounter with the serpent. In his Vulgate, Jerome omitted translating from either the Hebrew Bible or the Greek Septuagint the prepositional phrase which establishes Adam's presence. Jerome seems unwilling to accept that the representative male was unprotesting to the serpent. On the other hand, the King James Version, the Jewish Version of 1917, the New American Bible, the New International Version, and the New Jerusalem Bible do not overlook translating *immah* as "with her" in Genesis 3:6. Thus the composer pictures "her husband *with her*" when the fruit was stolen. Also, the plural verbs in the dialogue with the serpent suggest that Adam was present.

Here is how Gerhard von Rad, a famous biblical scholar, interprets Eve's role in Genesis 3:6:

> The woman is now alone. . . . The one who has been led astray now becomes a temptress. That is meant to indicate that the woman confronts the obscure allurements and mysteries that beset our limited life more directly than the man does. In the history of Yahweh-religion it has always been the women who have shown an inclination for obscure astrological cults.[5]

In contrast to this sexist and non sequitur comment, an early Christian writing views Adam and Eve differently:

> Why did the serpent not attack the man, rather than the woman? You say he went after her because she was the weaker of the two. On the contrary. In the transgression of the commandment, she showed herself to be the stronger . . . for she alone stood up to the serpent. She ate from the tree, but with resistance and dissent, and after being dealt with perfidiously. But Adam partook of the fruit given by the woman, without even beginning to make a fight.[6]

Jean Higgins, who resurrected this anonymous fragment from a neglected manuscript, has expressed her amusement over the Genesis 3 episode: "There is something comical in the image of the man standing there and never entering into the conversation at all, never intervening to stop the temptation, leaving the woman to do the talking, thinking, deciding, acting, and only at the end reaching out his hand to accept and eat what his wife put into his hands."[7] Phyllis Bird makes a more restrained comparison: "The woman in this portrait responds to the object of temptation intellectually and reflectively, employing both practical and esthetic judgment. The man, on the other hand, passively and unquestioningly accepts what the woman offers him."[8]

What the story does not say should also be noted. The composer approves of the pair clinging together in the nude prior to the serpent episode, so the forbidden fruit is not a symbol of sexual temptation. Their shame is from the loss of self-respect after stealing what did not belong to them, not from linking their loins in lustful embrace. Tikva Frymer-Kensky's perspective on Eve is based on the Genesis text: "Eve is portrayed as the spokesperson for the couple, and during her talk with the serpent she presents theological arguments. She is never portrayed as wanton, or as tempting or tempted sexually, nor does the biblical author single her out for greater blame than her partner."[9]

THE GREEK PANDORA

The myths of Pandora and Eve are similar in that both attempt to explain why woman was created. Hesiod's poetry, entitled *Theogony* and *Works and Days*, provides the only Greek source pertaining to woman's creation. He wrote about 700 B.C., probably a century or more after the recorder of the myth of Eve. Hesiod and the Hebrew writer were probably aware of oral traditions about human origins. Both may have known of stories of gods making humans of clay, a motif in earlier

Babylonian and Egyptian texts.[10] However, there is no evidence that the Greeks and Hebrews shared a common oral tradition pertaining to human creation. Actually the Greeks have a story of the creation of woman, but not of man.

Classics scholars suggest that Hesiod reversed the meaning of the name of an earth goddess called Pandora (all-giving) or Anesidora (one who sends up gifts). Vase paintings[11] and literary texts[12] give evidence of Pandora as a mother earth figure who was worshiped by some Greeks. The main English commentary on *Works and Days* states that Hesiod shows no awareness of the mythology of a divine Pandora-Anesidora giver of fertility.[13] Hence he made up a story of Pandora passively receiving gifts from the gods. While acknowledging a Pandora mythology older than Hesiod, Robert Graves states regarding Hesiod's tale: "Pandora is not a genuine myth, but an anti-feminist fable, probably of his own invention."[14] Jane Harrison sees in Hesiod's story evidence of a shift from matriarchy to patriarchy in Greek culture. As the life-bringing goddess Pandora is eclipsed, the death-bringing human Pandora arises.[15]

Woman, according to Hesiod, was created under the direction of father Zeus as retaliation against Prometheus. That trickster demigod had stolen heavenly fire for earthlings. The outwitted Zeus commissioned members of his pantheon to make "an evil thing in which men will all delight while they embrace their own destruction." Like a potter, crafts expert Hephaistos shaped a lump of clay into the shape of a luscious maiden; like a goldsmith, he made her a crown. Athena decked out this creation with clothes, jewelry, and flowers. Aphrodite bestowed charm and seductive powers, while Hermes implanted "a bitch's mind and a thief's temper." The "beautiful evil" (*kalon kakon*) was named Pandora because a variety of Olympian gods and goddesses had given her traits. This "booby trap" equipped with "lying and tricky talk" was delivered to Epimetheus ("afterthinker"), the uncautious brother of Prometheus ("forethinker"). Before Epimetheus accepted the gift, men lived like gods in a paradisiacal Golden Age "free from evils, harsh labor, and consuming diseases." But when Pandora maliciously opened the lid of a huge jar, all kinds of miseries flew out and infected mortals throughout the earth. Hesiod ends his story thus: "This was the origin of damnable womankind, a plague with which men must live." Further on in *Works and Days*, the poet warns of sweet-talking and hip-wiggling women who steal from those that find them fascinating. Hesiod's final judgment is this: "Any man who trusts a woman, trusts a deceiver."[16] He believed that the multitude of Pandora's daughters inherit their mothers' loveliness and cunningness. Their charm and breeding potentially compel men to associate with them, but their bad character makes domestic life miserable.

Hesiod expressed a hostility toward womankind that was endemic throughout Greek antiquity. G. L. Snider shows in his dissertation on the myth of Pandora that Homer's portrayal of women influenced Hesiod.[17] In the *Odyssey*, the soul of Agamemnon comments on Clytemnestra who stabbed him to death: "A bad name she gave to womankind, even to the best." The infidelity of his wife stimulates a reflection that has become proverbial: "Never trust a woman."[18] Hesiod's story of Pandora became a part of Greek education and youth thereby formed prejudices against women. *Works and Days* "was widely known and taught in various parts of Greece and the Aegean and thus exerted an influence on the moral and legal ideas of the centuries following Hesiod."[19]

Semonides, a younger contemporary of Hesiod, owed much to generalizations about women by Homer and Hesiod. In some passages these early poets assume that women are naturally a scourge because their evil actions come not from choice but from a divinely imposed fate. Satirist Semonides describes types of women in terms of seven different kinds of animals. He evaluates positively only those who are industrious like bees. He lampoons the rest, who are like filthy sows, yapping bitches, stubborn asses, wretched ferrets, vain mares, or tricky monkeys. Semonides concludes: "Zeus designed woman as the greatest of all evils. She is a source of evil, especially to her husband, even if she seems to be a help in some ways. No one manages to spend a whole day in contentment if he has a wife. . . . Yes, this is the greatest plague Zeus has made, and he has bound us to them with a fetter that cannot be broken. Because of this some have gone to Hades fighting for a woman."[20] Semonides is here probably thinking of the adulterous Helen of Troy.

Eva Cantarella, in a recent book entitled *Pandora's Daughters* in English translation, has combined sociological and literary scholarship in an examination of women's status in Greek antiquity. With some exaggeration of the evidence, she maintains that the misogyny articulated by Hesiod permeated the subsequent eras of Greek history. Cantarella concludes that Greeks throughout the ancient period "perpetuated a misogyny that excluded the female sex not only from social and political life but also from the world of reason, and consequently from that of love."[21]

Can literary fragments be relied on to portray dominant cultural values? If so, the characteristic ancient Greek outlook on women can be found in two quips by comic playwrights. Eubulus, a fourth-century Athenian, judging evil women to outnumber good ones overwhelmingly, alludes to Pandora. "The second man to marry should be punished, but not the first [Epimetheus], who had no experience of how awful a wife can be."[22] Eva Keuls, in her study of sexual politics in ancient Athens, selects this line from the fifth-century Pherecrates to illustrate the deep-seated misogyny: "He who bemoans the death of his wife is a fool who doesn't appreciate his good fortune."[23]

THE JEWISH/CHRISTIAN EVE

Hellenization impacted Western Asia after the conquests of Alexander in the fourth century. The Greek theme of women being universally alluring but inherently disastrous infiltrated Jewish thought after Palestine came under Hellenistic control. In the Hebrew Bible the best example of what the French would call *la femme fatale* is found in Ecclesiastes 7:26. In that verse a philosopher sounds a warning about the wiles of all women: "I found something more bitter than death—woman. The love she offers you will catch you like a trap or like a net; and her arms around you will hold you like a chain. A man who pleases God can get away, but she will catch the sinner." In the Israelite society prior to the Hellenistic era, there were proverbs and stories about prostitutes and nagging wives who could precipitate a calamity, but such women were usually denounced in order to heighten the contrast with virtuous women.

The Pandora motif was transferred to the Eve myth in Jewish writing after the era of the Hebrew Bible and before Christianity arose. Philo, who absorbed the Hellenistic culture of Alexandria, projects onto the Hebrew Bible alien Greek ideas. His references to the poems of Hesiod show that he must have been acquainted with the Pandora myth. Hence, in his commentary on Genesis, woman is singled out as "the beginning of evil." Eve and her daughters are described in this disparaging way: "The woman, being imperfect and depraved by nature, made the beginning of sinning and prevaricating; but the man, being the more excellent and perfect creature, was the first to set the example of blushing and of being ashamed, and indeed of every good feeling and action."[24]

The Greek text of The Life of Adam and Eve, probably written in the first century of the Christian era, retells the Eden story in order to stress Eve's culpability. In that Jewish midrash, published now in *The Old Testament Pseudepigrapha*, Eve explains to her children what she did after eating the forbidden fruit:

> I cried out with a loud voice, saying, "Adam, Adam, where are you? Rise, come to me and I will show you a great mystery.". . . When he came, I opened my mouth and the

devil was speaking, and I began to admonish him, saying, "Come, my lord Adam, listen to me and eat of the fruit of the tree of which God told us not to eat from, and you shall be as God." Your father answered and said, "I fear lest God be angry with me." And I said to him, "Do not fear; for as soon as you eat, you shall know good and evil." Then I quickly persuaded him. He ate, and his eyes were opened, and he also realized his nakedness. And he said to me, "O evil woman! Why have you wrought destruction among us? You have estranged me from the glory of God."[25]

The midrash also says that Eve denounced a beast for attacking her son Seth and for not being in subjection to those made in the image of God. The beast replied that Eve's sin caused the animals to revolt. After she greedily ate the forbidden fruit, the nature of beasts was transformed.[26]

Rabbinical Judaism accepted the Pseudepigrapha's degrading view of Eve. To justify punishments directed toward women, the Palestinian Talmud offers this invidious comparison: "Adam was the light of the world . . . and Eve was the cause of his death."[27]

Dora and Erwin Panofsky, in their valuable study of the Pandora motif in Western literature and art, show that Christian leaders had more interest in Pandora than pagan Roman writers. "The Fathers of the Church are more important for the transmission — and transformation — of the myth of Pandora than the secular writers; in an attempt to corroborate the doctrine of original sin by a classical parallel, yet to oppose Christian truth to pagan fable, they likened her to Eve."[28]

Tertullian, the first leader of Latin Christianity, compared the biblical and Greek stories of the first woman. Eve only differs from Pandora, he notes, in that she is "encircled with leaves about the middle than with flowers about the temple."[29] His infamous denunciation of women displays his mixture of the two myths:

Do you not know that each of you is an Eve? God's sentence on your gender lives even in our times and so it is necessary that the guilt must also continue. You are the one who opened the devil's door; you unsealed the forbidden tree; you first betrayed the divine law; you are the one who enticed him whom the devil was too weak to attack. How easily you destroyed man, the image of God! Because of the death which you brought upon us, even the Son of God had to die.[30]

Opening the devil's door and unsealing the forbidden tree are images similar to Pandora's raising the lid of a jar containing the earth's evils. After quoting this passage from Tertullian, Paul Jewett writes, "As in ancient Greek mythology Pandora opened the fateful box, so in Christian thought it was Eve, the first woman, who ruined mankind."[31] John Phillips shows the way in which Eve's alleged fatal curiosity becomes a prominent motif in European folk tales. He attributes this "relatively late diagnosis of woman's special weakness" to confusing Eve with Pandora.[32]

Tertullian thought of Eve and Pandora as the archetype of temptresses who ruin men by their good looks. He implores Christian women to deface their beauty in order to avoid stimulating male sexual desire. Not only must cosmetics and attractive clothing be abhorred but "even natural grace must be obliterated by concealment and negligence."[33] Wearing a veil when going into public places helps to mortify the flesh. Tertullian asks: "Who will have the audacity to intrude with his eyes upon a shrouded face? a face without feeling? a face, so to say, morose?"[34] Men's virtue is least threatened if women stay secluded. "Busy your hands with spinning," Tertullian writes; "keep your feet at home."[35]

John Chrysostom (literally, "golden mouth") and Gregory Nazianzen, outstanding fourth-century leaders of Greek Christianity, thought of Eve as an ensnarer. Hesiod would have liked Chrysostom's description of the daughters of Eve: "How often do we, from beholding a woman, suffer a thousand evils. . . . The beauty of women is the greatest snare. . . . Let us then discern the snares, and walk far off from them! Let us discern the precipices, and not even approach them!"[36] Although Chrysostom did not explicitly refer to Hesiod's lovely curse, he provided later witch-hunters with this eloquent portrait of Pandora alias Eve: "What else is woman but a foe to friendship, an inescapable punishment, a necessary evil, a natural temptation, a desirable calamity, a domestic danger, a delectable detriment, an evil of nature, painted with fair colors!"[37] Chrysostom had followed the Hesiodic tradition in alleging a gap between a woman's attractive appearance and her horrible nature. Gregory Nazianzen, Archbishop of Constantinople, interpreted Eve as the devil's advocate: "Instead of an assistant, she became an enemy . . . beguiling the man by means of pleasure."[38]

Medieval Christians were so ignorant of Greek mythology that Pandora disappears until scholars rediscovered classical pagan texts. Jean Cousin's *Eva Prima Pandora* makes explicit the mythological confusion that was common in the sixteenth century. He paints a lovely, nearly nude body with a snake coiled around her left arm. Her right hand, ominously resting on a skull, holds a sprig from the forbidden tree. Behind Eve/Pandora is an open vase from which vapors are escaping.[39]

Renaissance scholar Erasmus converted Pandora's storage jar (*pithos*) into a box (*pyxis*) by confusing a detail from the Greek story with an episode in Roman literature when retelling the story of the Prototypical woman. A comment from Bishop Jean Oliver's sixteenth-century book entitled *Pandora* illustrates the way in which Erasmus's box mistranslation became accepted in most modern European languages. "Eve in Scripture opened the forbidden fruit by her bite, by which death invaded the world. So did Pandora open the box in defiance of a divine injunction, whereby all the evils and infinite calamities broke loose and overwhelmed the hapless mortals with countless infirmities."[40]

John Milton blended his thorough knowledge of classical

mythology with Christian tradition in extolling the original
human creation. "A consummate and most adorned Pandora
was bestow'd upon Adam," he writes.[41] The Puritan poet im-
agines the Greek and Hebrew primal women as alike except
that Eve is "more lovely than Pandora, whom the Gods en-
dowed with all their gifts." She "ensnar'd mankind with her fair
looks, to be aveng'd on him who had stole Jove's authentic
fire."[42] In Book 9 of *Paradise Lost* Milton develops Augustine's
heroic Adam interpretation. At the time of the encounter with
the serpentine incarnation of Satan, Eve is laboring in Eden at
a place separated from Adam. He had urged her to stay under
his protection by his side but she stubbornly wanted to work in-
dependently. On learning that credulous Eve has succumbed
to the flattering tempter and has become a surrogate serpent,
Adam is horrified. He then indulges in eating the forbidden
fruit against his better judgment because he is willing to die
bound to his spouse. The moral superiority of self-sacrificial
Adam stands out in bold relief against the deadly delight of
Eve.

The Eve/Pandora composite is now embedded in Western
secular literature. Anatole France, a leading figure in modern
French literature, remarked that the location of hell was unknown
until Tertullian discovered its gate "between the legs of women."[43]
In a bestseller, Philip Wylie concludes his diatribe against the
power of American women by comparing them to Pandora and
"the mother of Cain."[44] English writer Geoffrey Ashe calls Eve a
"troublemaker" who "appears in Genesis as a Hebrew Pandora,
the villainess in a story about the origin of human misfortune."[45]
Nikos Kazantzakis's most famous character views women as did
his Greek literary ancestor. Even as Hesiod called Pandora "a
booby-trap," so Zorba warns: "No matter where you touch a
woman, you touch the devil's horns. Beware of her, my boy! She
also stole the apples in the garden of Eden; she shoved them down
her bodice, and now she goes out and about, strutting all over the
place. A plague on her! Eat any of those apples and you're lost;
don't eat any and you'll still be lost!"[46]

Actually, as biblical scholar Bruce Vawter rightly observes: "Genesis does not share in the motif common in ancient mythologies according to which a woman was the cause of the miseries of a disordered world ('Pandora's Box' is a familiar example)."[47] Indeed, the ancient storyteller seems to regard Adam's attempt to hide behind his wife as ludicrous buck passing. Regarding this perennially popular rationalization, some wag has quipped: Adam took it like a man and blamed his wife! He attempted to excuse his own bad choice by complaining to God about having to eat what his wife served him. Suffragette Lillie Blake commented on Genesis 3:12: " 'The woman thou gavest to be with me, she gave me and I did eat,' he whines — trying to shield himself at his wife's expense! Again we are amazed that upon such a story men have built up a theory of their superiority!"[48]

Exonerating one gender at the expense of the other is a pernicious scapegoating procedure that has been going on all too long. Hopefully the corrective exegesis in our times, done mainly by female scholars, will bring an end to this denigration. Male prejudice toward women is difficult to kill but a fresh look at the myth of Eve provides no reinforcement for keeping it alive.

Chapter 4

The Fall and Woman

BIBLICAL INTERPRETATIONS

"Fall," as used in Christian theology, conveys the idea of a precipitous plunge into the abyss of damnation. Humans are presumed to be like the fallen Humpty Dumpty, who cannot become a whole egg again and develop into a mature bird despite the massive efforts of royal horses and men. The Fall of the first humans is irreparable so their descendants cannot ascend from depravity to innocence.

This image of the Fall, and the "Sinned we all" rhyme, is etched so indelibly in the Christian's psyche that most commentaries interpret Genesis 3 as the story of mankind's Fall. As commonly assumed, the necessity of a God-man savior is predicated upon the Fall of a woman and then the Fall of her spouse. However, Hebrew or Greek words translatable as *fall* do not occur in the Bible in reference to Adam and Eve. There is no foundation in the Garden of Eden story for doctrines of original sin, inherited guilt, or total depravity which allegedly infect all humans. What then has given rise to this basic belief among most Christians?

As we have noted, the Eden story is about the human misuse of moral freedom and the consequential penalties. Yahweh gives the man a life sentence at hard labor on marginal farmland; the woman is given pain in childbirth and domination by her husband. Such suffering is no more part of divine

intentionality than the homicide and slavery featured in subsequent chapters of Genesis. These societal patterns are not
sanctified as a necessary accommodation for fallen human nature. All are an avoidable result of human unfaithfulness to the
created order.

Interpreters have frequently but erroneously presumed that
the Genesis storyteller was describing what ought to be a continual divine penalty to humankind for the sin of our first
parents. The so-called *Apostolic Constitutions,* for example,
quotes "He shall rule over you" from Genesis 3:16 to prove that
woman's inferiority is part of the "order of creation."[1] But
myths are ahistorical and do not attempt to chronicle the past
or predict the future. Rather, they attempt to explain the
present situation. Alienation from Yahweh causes disharmony
in earthly associations. Work is no longer a pleasant activity as
intended but a grim struggle with nature. The maternal toil to
insure biological survival becomes harsh when a tyrannical husband replaces a companion in marriage.

Some contemporary scholars have clarified what the adamic
myth was not trying to convey. In a doctoral dissertation,
George Riggan points out: "There is in Genesis 3 no doctrine
of a catastrophic change in human nature, no physical or moral
Fall in the technical sense, no idea of seminal or metaphysical
inclusion of the race in Adam, no doctrine of original sin."[2]
Theologian Paul Tillich treats the Eden story as a symbol of
estrangement while separating it entirely from a historical context. He writes: "The notion of a moment in time in which man
and nature were changed from good to evil is absurd, and it has
no foundations in experience or revelation."[3]

In the Hebrew Bible, the Adam and Eve story is never used
as an explanation for evil. While that ancient literary collection
says much about oppressive relationships among humans, it
does not blame these "sins" on their first parents having shattered the divine image. Indeed, the death penalty is decreed
for murder in Genesis 9 because "the image of God" is still
present in humans. There is no mention of its loss elsewhere in

the Hebrew Bible. Notions of a calamitous drop in human status cannot be traced to the teachings of the Hebrew prophets and priests, even though they were profoundly conscious of the depth of human sin and the social transmission of human evil. Postbiblical Jewish writers, impacted by Hellenistic misogyny, introduced some ingredients for what would become the Judeo-Christian Fall doctrine. Jesus ben Sirach, living in the second century before the Christian era, was the first to attribute the reign of death to a happening in Eden. Exempting his fellow males from responsibility, he states: "From a woman sin began, and through her we all die." His wisdom poem, written in Greek, also makes this invidious comparison: "A man's wickedness is better than a woman's goodness; it is woman who brings shame and disgrace."[4]

The Testament of Reuben, written about the same time as the Wisdom of Sirach, expands the misogynistic theme:

Women are evil, my children. . . . They scheme treacherously how they might entice men to themselves by means of their looks. . . . The angel of the Lord told me, and taught me, that women are overcome by the spirit of fornication more than men, and in their heart they plot against men; and by means of their adornment they deceive first their minds, and by the glance of the eye they implant their poison, and finally they take them captive. . . . They allured the watchers who were before the flood. . . . The women lusted after the watchers who reached even unto heaven and then gave birth to giants.[5]

Here it is alleged that the women referred to in Genesis 6 seduced the angelic "watchers" by means of their alluring cosmetics. Assuming that noncorporeal creatures cannot procreate, this embellishment describes the presence of angels in the minds of women as they engage in marital intercourse with their husbands. Because they lusted after the "sons of God," the wives conceive monstrous offspring.

Enoch, another second-century book, also relies on Genesis

6 rather than Genesis 3 for explaining the beginning of sin. This intertestamental writing is closer to the original, for the sons of God initiate the affairs and there is no problem in sons of God having physical intercourse with earthlings and procreating. After many wayward angels descent from heaven to have relations with beautiful women, miscegenation occurs. The giants who are produced bring much destruction to the earth. The women who are in liaison with the fallen angels become sirens after learning from them wicked ways of ornamenting themselves.

The New Testament does not record Jesus as speaking of matters related to an alleged Fall and there is no basis in the Gospels for blaming the daughters of Eve for evil in the world. On the contrary, Jesus idealized the Eden story of marital partnership.[6] He hoped for a rejection of the prevailing patriarchal pattern of divorce and for a return to the relationship described in Genesis 2. In the authentic letters of the apostle Paul, the origin of sin is not associated with one gender. "Sin came into the world through one human [Greek, *anthropos*]," according to Romans 5:12. The apostle uses the name "Adam" to designate the representative head of sinful humanity, but not to distinguish the first male human from the first female. As I have demonstrated elsewhere, Paul did not believe that Adam's sin had resulted in a congenital moral deformity.[7] He did not believe that humans fail to live as God intended, but this is due to wrong individual choices.

A letter to Timothy, attributed to Paul but probably written some decades after his death, provides the Christian Bible's first and only invidious blaming of Eve more than her mate. It starkly asserts: "I permit no woman to teach or to have authority over men; she is to keep silent. For Adam was formed first, then Eve; and Adam was not deceived, but the woman was deceived and became a transgressor."[8] The consensus of current scholarly interpretation of this passage is well summarized by Rosemary Ruether: "The teachings of 1 Timothy about women keeping silence appear, not as the uniform position of the New Testament Church, but as a second generation reaction against widespread participation of women in leadership, teaching and ministering in first-generation Christianity."[9] The pseudepigraphal letter then declares — quite contrary to Paul's doctrine — that the work of bearing children was necessary for a woman's salvation. The 1 Timothy eisegesis of the Genesis text and perversion of Paul's teaching became the basis for subsequent churchmen declaring that women are more susceptible to sin than men and therefore only the morally stronger male can be ordained. Church leaders refused to extend sacred offices to the gender alleged to be last in the order of creation but first in the order of sin.

CHURCH VIEWPOINTS

As this survey will display, a continual theme in Christianity from the second century onward has been that women are more responsible than men for the debilitating evil that permeates life. Christian writers borrowed a scurrilous Jewish tale which attributes the birth of Cain to Eve's seduction by the serpent in Eden.[10] In an influential apocryphal Gospel, Joseph on learning of Mary's pregnancy, initially responds in this manner: "Has the story of Adam been repeated in me? For as Adam was absent in the hour of his prayer and the serpent came and found Eve alone and deceived and defiled her, so also has it happened to me."[11] Apologist Justin imagined that Eve's mind was impregnated by the seminal ideas of Satan, but a second Eve came later to rescue humanity. "Eve, an undefiled virgin, conceived the word of the serpent and brought forth disobedience and death. But the virgin Mary . . . gave birth to him . . . by whom God destroys the serpent."[12]

Bishop Irenaeus, the most formidable defender of Christianity in the second century, developed the Eve-Mary typology in which sexual abstinence becomes prominent as a means of salvation. "Eve became disobedient and was made the cause of death both to herself and to the entire race."[13] Virginal Mary and her virginal son restore the damage begun by Eve.

Greek Bishop Chrysostom declared: "Woman taught once and ruined all. . . . What happened to the first woman occasioned the subjection of the whole sex."[14] Chrysostom claimed that Eve's wily nature was well displayed in Bathsheba. When his friend Theodore became betrothed, Chrysostom wrote: "If you consider what is contained in beautiful eyes, a straight nose, a mouth, and cheeks, you will agree that a well-shaped body is merely a whitewashed tomb; the parts within are full of filth. . . . The blessed David also had a fall like that which has now happened to you."[15] Chrysostom's inversion of the biblical story of David's seduction of Bathsheba became a staple of medieval sermons.[16]

The slander against Eve which Justin transmitted from Jewish lore was carried by Tertullian into Western Christianity. He wrote: "Let no one say that Eve conceived nothing in her womb at the devil's word. The devil's word was the seed for her so that afterward she should give birth as an outcast and bring forth in sorrow. In fact, she gave birth to a devil who murdered his brother."[17] In the Judeo-Christian tradition, mother Eve is more identified with wicked Cain than righteous Abel.

According to Jerome, one of the most famous of all biblical translators and interpreters, "Ava" was Gabriel's greeting to Mary because the Nazareth virgin reversed the bad name of "Eva," the sexual siren of Eden. He counseled, "Always bear in mind that it was a woman who expelled the tiller of Paradise from his heritage."[18]

Marina Warner finds in these church fathers an unwitting tribute to those they denounce. She writes: "The fury unleashed against Eve and all her kind is almost flattering, so exaggerated is the picture of women's fatal and all-powerful charms and men's incapacity to resist."[19]

Bishop Augustine, the most influential leader in the whole course of Western Christendom, gave a distinctive focus to the Garden of Eden story. As theologian Paul Lehmann observes, "Augustine went further than any Christian thinker in connecting human sexuality with the Fall."[20] Due in large part to his personal guilt feelings over illicit sexual pleasures when a young man, Augustine came to assume that the sexual urge was evil in itself. He is largely responsible for *concupiscentia* – a neutral term in classical Latin meaning strong desire – coming to mean evil lust in subsequent Catholic doctrine.[21] Also he was among the first to equate concupiscence with "original sin."[22]

Augustine postulated that sexual desire could not have been a part of God's perfect creation. How then could reproduction have occurred? Had there been no original sin, Augustine fantasized, Adam would have impregnated Eve while relaxing passionlessly on her bosom. While operating under complete rational control Adam would cooly have summoned his semen forth and, without hymenal impairment, it would have dripped down into her vagina.[23] "Away with the thought that there should have been . . . any unregulated excitement," Augustine insisted.[24]

To show that it is plausible to think of humans having complete physical control in an uncorrupted condition, Augustine tells of the power some individuals have over particular bodily parts. Just as some people now can deliberately "make their ears move, either one at a time or both together," and others "can make musical notes issue from their bowels so as to produce a musical effect," so "our organs without the excitement of concupiscence could have obeyed human will for all the purposes of parenthood."[25]

Only after indulging in sin was Adam unable to keep his penis from acting up. Like an ass rebelling against training, it would not respond to its owner's commands.[26] Augustine thought Adam received an appropriate penalty for willful disobedience to the fruit tree prohibition in having his penis become likewise disobedient to his will. Adam, who had previously been naked and unashamed, now is highly embarrassed at the "bestial motion" of his penis.[27] Indeed, blushing is alleged to have originated from Adam's chagrin over penile perversity.[28] He quickly covers his loins in order to conceal from others his lack of self-mastery.[29] Power over the penis is lost forever to Adam's offspring and henceforth its arousal and its orgasm will often be triggered by someone else. Eve as well as Adam was conscience-stricken by her involuntary sexual impulses. "The motion of their bodily members," Augustine writes, "released the shocking news of their indecent nakedness, made them notice it, and gave them shame."[30]

Augustine maintained that all humans who have been conceived by sexual intercourse inherit from Adam unruly genitals. "Behold the place!" he exclaimed. "That's the place from which the first sin was passed on."[31] He informed men in his congregation that each could witness the effect of the Fall in his penis's disobedience to authoritative command. The corrupted semen ejaculated from the faulty member would contaminate the next generation by what we call genes. Augustine thought the evil sexual impulse is transmitted in the same physiological way as children inherit the skin pigmentation of their parents.[32]

Augustine found evidence of the perpetual shameful consequence of Adam's sin in the fact that couples, even when bound in legal wedlock, dread engaging in intercourse except in a dark place. "Even shameless men call this shameful," Augustine claimed; "and though they love the pleasure, they dare not display it."[33] Consequently, married partners "seek out secret retreats for cohabitation, and dare not have even the children whom they have themselves begotten to be witnesses of what they do."[34]

While admitting that sexual consummation produces "the greatest of all bodily pleasures,"[35] Augustine believes it is dishonorable for Christians to seek sexual pleasure even within marriage. Marital coitus can be performed without committing "venial" sin only if spouses are exclusively motivated by a grim determination to propagate.[36] "Since you cannot reproduce in any other way," he laments, "you must descend against your will to this punishment of Adam."[37] The celibate bishop advises a man to love his wife as he loves his enemy — he should accept both as creatures of God but hate what makes them corrupt. With respect to his spouse, a husband should hate her desire for sexual pleasure.[38] In his several treatises on marriage, the sexual act as a symbolic expression of devoted love is nowhere regarded as even a secondary purpose of marriage. Augustine argues that it is wrong for married couples who do not hope for conception to have sexual union even as it is wrong for a person to consume food in excess of what is necessary for survival.[39]

To renounce sexual intercourse entirely is to hasten the coming of the perfected City of God.[40] Consequently Augustine praises those already bound in matrimony who have vowed "to observe a perpetual abstinence from the use of carnal concupiscence."[41] Likewise he commends the supererogation of virginal men and women who impose upon themselves the command, "Thou shalt not wed."[42]

Augustine regarded Jesus as the second Adam because, like the first Adam before his Fall, he had no sexual drive. The bishop believed that God effected this unique exception to the rest of humanity by miraculously enabling a woman to become fertilized without receiving the contaminated semen of Adam's descendants.[43] Whereas the first Adam was "able not to sin," Jesus, because of his virginal conception, was "not able to sin."[44]

In Augustine's scheme of sin and salvation, man's rambunctious private parts become proof of his being conceived in iniquity and normally destined for the torment of hell. Jesus, the lustless Savior, rescues some whom otherwise would receive their just damnation. Those few whom God elects show their appreciation by attempting to imitate Jesus' alleged lifestyle. Augustine's doctrine did much to attract guilt-stricken individuals to medieval monasteries, for sexual discipline was prominently featured there.

Augustine explained how the New Testament could state that both Adam and Eve sinned even though only Eve was deceived. "The woman accepted as true what the serpent told her, but the man could not bear to be severed from his only companion, even though this involved a partnership in sin."[45] Although Adam would have preferred not to eat the forbidden fruit, he gallantly ate "with his eyes open" to avoid vexing his wife. From this biblical story Augustine extracts this moral for men: "Whether it is in a wife or a mother, it is still Eve the temptress that we must beware of in any woman."[46] Satan did not remove Job's wife when tormenting Job, Augustine believed, because the devil learned from his success with Eve that a woman was an able assistant.[47]

According to Augustine, the Genesis flood as well as the Fall of the first human parents was occasioned by woman. Viewing women as incarnations of sensuality, he claimed that they seduced the angelic sons of God. It was their "depraved morals" and "bodily beauty" that brought on that second calamity.[48]

The misogyny of the church fathers encouraged even more exaggerated contempt for women in the Middle Ages. In Ireland this testimony circulated: "I am Eve, the wife of noble Adam; . . . it was I who robbed my children of heaven; it is I by right who should have been crucified. . . . There would be no hell, there would be no grief, there would be no terror but for me."[49] *Mystere d'Adam*, one of the earliest morality plays, depicts Eve as lacking a conscience. Adam is unable to convince her that the Devil is treacherous. Although vexed at his wife's eating the forbidden fruit, her persistent nagging causes him to capitulate to her offer.[50]

A witch-angel polarity emerged in attitudes toward women during the medieval period. The sexually active were often associated with the underworld devil while those with unruptured hymens were adored on a par with heavenly angels. *Vir*gins had *vir*tue because, as the roots of these words indicate, they had male (Latin, *vir*) restraint. In the Marian cult, the exalted "Queen of Heaven" set in bolder relief "witches" who, by means of satanic voluptuousness, enchained mortals for consignment to hell.

In the fourteenth century, the faculty of the University of Bologna decreed that the academic community should avoid female contacts because "woman is the fountain of sin, the weapon of the devil, the cause of man's banishment from Paradise."[51] At that same time the priest in *The Canterbury Tales* taught:

> Woman's counsel brought us first to woe,
> And made Adam from Paradise to go.[52]

Chaucer's Wife of Bath recalls clerical libel on her sex and speculates on what would have happened if scribes were not male:

> If women had but written stories;
> As have these clerks within their oratories,
> They would have written of men more wickedness
> Than all the race of Adam could redress.[53]

The most vigorous attack on women by the church was launched by theology professors Heinrich Kramer and James Sprenger. In 1484, Pope Innocent VIII appointed them as inquisitors for the purpose of stamping out alleged witches. In their manual for detecting and punishing them, they direct readers to the primal pattern for women: "The Scriptures have much that is evil to say about women, and this because of the first temptress, Eve, and her imitators. . . . Eve seduced Adam . . . therefore she is more bitter than death."[54] *The Hammer Against Witches*, the title of Kramer and Sprenger's work of quintessential misogyny, "was the ultimate, irrefutable, unarguable authority" wherever witchcraft trials were held. Its popularity over the centuries is attested by the fact that it has gone through dozens of editions since it was first published in 1486. Even though it is as bigoted as Hitler's *Mein Kampf*, Montague Summers, a prominent witchcraft researcher and a twentieth-century Catholic priest, judges it as "among the most important, wisest, and weightiest books in the world."[55] The book provided the rationalization for torturing and executing many thousands of women.[56]

The fifteenth-century Catholic witchmania infected Protestantism in the subsequent two centuries. Trevor Davies, in a well-documented study, has demonstrated that "the Protestant Reformers were even more zealous witch-hunters than the Roman Catholics themselves."[57] Presbyterian reformer John Knox wrote an inflammatory tract entitled *The First Blast of the Trumpet Against the Monstrous Regimen of Women*. Having contempt for independent women regardless of their high or low position, Knox denounced reigning queens and alleged witches.[58] In support of his position he quoted what Augustine had written: "A woman ought to do service unto her husband as unto God."[59] Acting as a spokesman for God, Knox delivered this message to women:

> Forasmuch as thou hast abused thy former condition, and because thy free will hath brought thy selfe and mankind into the bondage of Satan, I therefore will bring thee in bondage to man. For where before thy obedience should have been voluntarie, nowe it shall be by constreint and by necessitie; and that because thou hast deceived thy man, thou shalt therefore be no longer maistress over thine own appetites, over thine owne will or desires. For in thee there is nether reason nor discretion whiche be able to moderate thy affections, and therefore they shall be subject to the desire of thy man. He shall be Lord and Governour, not onlie over thy bodie, but even over thy appetites and will.[60]

A generation after Knox there was another powerful preacher in Britain who echoed both the biography and the ideas of Augustine. John Donne, the Dean of St. Paul's Cathedral in London, states:

> I preach but the sense of Gods indignation upon mine own soul. . . . I only gather into my memory, and powr out in

the presence of my God, and his Church, the sinfull history of mine own *youth*. . . . In the generation of *our parents*, we were *conceiv'd in sin*; that is, they sinn'd in that . . . very act of generation, because then we became in part the subject of *Originall sin*. . . . In the very first minute of our life, in our quickning in our mothers womb, wee become guilty of *Adams* sin done 6000 years before.[61]

Renaissance culture carried forward another aspect of Augustine's antifeminism. Erasmus provides this allegorical comment: "That slimy snake, the first betrayer of our peace and the father of restlessness, never ceases to watch and lie in wait beneath the heel of woman, whom he once poisoned. By 'woman' we mean, of course, the carnal or sensual part of man. For this is our Eve, through whom the crafty serpent entices and lures our minds to deadly pleasures."[62]

Were one limited to Renaissance art for understanding the Eden story, one might presume that Eve was created in the image of the primeval serpent. Bearing the torso of a human female, Michelangelo's Sistine Chapel serpent is entwined about the forbidden tree while handing fruit to Eve. Other artists of that period followed Michelangelo's lead and portrayed Eve as similar in appearance to the evil serpent, who could stand erect. German Protestant Hans Baldung Grien painted a wily-eyed and grinning Eve playing with the serpent's phalliclike tail.

CONTEMPORARY OUTLOOKS

The shadow of Augustine remains over twentieth-century theology, even though the sexism is less pronounced. In 1968, Pope Paul declared: "The original offense committed by Adam caused human nature, common to all men, to fall to a state in which it bears the consequences of that offense, and which is not the state in which it was at first in our first parents. . . . We therefore hold, with the Council of Trent, that original sin is transmitted with human nature 'not by imitation, but by propagation.' "63 Catholic R. F. Trevett, begins his discussion of sex with the categorical assertion: "If there was no Fall, Christianity is nonsense." Trevett goes on to show how "man's total subsequent evolution – and this includes his sex life – was altered by the fact of the Fall."64

Many Protestants continue to accept the dogma of total depravity. Those in the Calvinist tradition endorse a seventeenth-century doctrinal statement regarding Adam and Eve:

> They fell from their original righteousness and communion with God, and so became dead in sin and wholly defiled in all the faculties and parts of soul and body. They being the root of all mankind, the guilt of this sin was imputed, and the same death in sin and corrupted nature conveyed to all their posterity, descending from them by ordinary generation. From this original corruption, whereby we are utterly indisposed, disabled, and made opposite to all good, and wholly inclined to all evil, do proceed all actual transgressions.65

A sampling of American clergy in the Lutheran tradition shows that most of them believe that "all persons are born with natures wholly perverse, sinful, and depraved" because they are offspring of the disobedient Adam and Eve.66

S. H. Kellogg, a Protestant biblical expositor, tells of "the extreme evil of the state of sin into which the first woman, by that first sin, brought all womanhood." Kellogg asserts that "the specific curse denounced against the woman, as recorded in the book of Genesis, is no dead letter, but a fact. . . . She can only bring forth another sinful creature like herself; and if a daughter, then a daughter inheriting all her own peculiar infirmities and disabilities."67 Some Protestants objected to anesthetics for women in labor because "the pangs of childbirth was her curse for original sin."68

The Unification Church of Sun Myung Moon, a spin-off of the Protestant missionary movement in Korea, claims that the fundamental sin of Eden was Eve's domination of Adam after being dominated by the devil.[69] Her witchcraft is described in the official doctrine of the "Moonies":

> Eve's fall consisted of two kinds of illicit love affairs. The first one was the spiritual fall through love with the archangel [Lucifer]. The second was the physical fall through love with Adam. . . . Cain and Abel were the fruits of Eve's illicit love. . . . Eve's sin formed the root of all sin.[70]

Eve has been so closely associated with sin that one might think that her name is the etymological root of evil! "Exorcising Evil from Eve" is a chapter title in one of Mary Daly's women's liberation books.[71] She contends that over the millennia Eve has been continually viewed as the universal woman and as the incarnation of evil. John Phillips has analyzed the Eve motif in the works of artists, theologians, and psychologists across the ages. He believes that the story of Eve is "at the heart of the concept of woman in Western civilization." "She becomes through her weaker nature the instrument of evil," he concludes.[72]

Many interpreters, including Daly and Phillips, have unfairly transferred interpretations of some influential church leaders to a Hebrew myth. Eve has been persistently but wrongly thought of in Western culture as the lovely but treacherous specimen of femininity who unleashed wickedness. The Genesis text has been twisted to mean that Adam's uppity wife caused the downfall of her noble spouse and that every woman reflects the image of her primeval counterpart.

Caricaturing the vindictiveness of bigots, A. E. Housman writes:

> When Adam day by day
> Woke up in Paradise,
> He always used to say
> "Oh, this is very nice."

> But Eve from scenes of bliss
> Transported him for life.
> The more I think of this
> The more I beat my wife.

Some churchmen are less amusing for they are serious in their attempts to ridicule and subordinate women. The most striking recent example of perverse caricaturing of Eve is found in the largest Protestant denomination in the United States. In 1984 the Southern Baptist Convention approved a resolution presented by Carl Henry, the former editor of *Christianity Today*, which states in effect that women are cursed by Eve. Thousands of delegates agreed that women should be excluded from ordination because "man was first in creation and woman was first in the Edenic fall."[73]

Two assessments of the church's heritage pertaining to "original sin" provide an appropriate conclusion to this survey. French philosopher Paul Ricoeur writes: "The harm that has been done to souls, during the centuries of Christianity, first by the literal interpretation of the story of Adam, and then by the confusion of this myth, treated as history, with later speculations, principally Augustinian, about original sin, will never be adequately told."[74] American psychologist Harry Overstreet sounds a similar note:

> We might almost say that the curse which, through all subsequent centuries, has rested upon man came, not from Adam, but from Augustine. To a peculiar degree, it was Augustine who denied to our species the healthy blessing of self-respect.... What we had from Jesus of Nazareth was an invitation to maturity injected into the immature Roman world. That world could not understand his mature insight.... If Christian religion could have gone on straight from this point, it would doubtless today be a vastly different thing from what it is. Instead, a few centuries later...Adam's disobedience became a more important reality than man's potential love of God and his neighbor.[75]

Chapter 5

Jesus and Creation

INCARNATION THEMES

A gynomorphic motif was prominent in ancient Jewish creation theology. Wisdom was personified as a woman, called Hokmah in Hebrew, or Sophia in Greek. A soliloquy in the book of Proverbs tells of her being God's constant companion at the world's creation:

> Happy is the person who has found Hokmah . . . for the gain she brings is better than gold. . . . She is a tree of life to all who grasp her, and those who hold her fast are safe. . . . Yahweh possessed me at the beginning of his works, before all else was made. . . . I was there when he set the heavens in their place, when he put an arch over the ocean, . . . when he prescribed its limits and knit together earth's foundations. I was at this side each day, his darling and delight, playing in his presence continually.[1]

The Wisdom of Solomon gives this fuller description:

> She is a breath of the power of God and a pure revelation of the glory of the Almighty. . . . She is a reflection of the everlasting light, a spotless mirror of the activity of God. . . . Herself unchanging, she renews everything. In

every generation she enters into holy persons, making
them friends of God and prophets. . . . She is more radiant
than the sun. She reaches from one end of the earth to the
other, and orders all things well.[2]

Given this theological heritage, it is understandable that
some New Testament writers associate Sophia with the
founder of Christianity. The apostle Paul designates Christ as
Theou Sophia, God's Wisdom.[3] According to that first Christian theologian, the lowly Jesus personifies Sophia by making
intimate the lofty Ultimate. The figure of Sophia functions for
Paul much as the Logos in the prologue of the Fourth Gospel.
Accordingly, in the beginning was Sophia and she became in-
carnate in Jesus. Also, the Synoptic Gospels state that Jesus
viewed John the Baptist and himself as inspired by Sophia.
After pointing out that differing prophetic voices have their
place in the divine scheme, he concludes, "Sophia is proved
right by all her children."[4]

Jesus also incarnated a feminine attribute of God alluded to
in Genesis. In the opening scene of the Bible, the Spirit (female
gender) is pictured as fluttering over the primeval waters. To
extend the metaphor, as in Deuteronomy 32:11, the Spirit
hatches out of the cosmic egg and hovers over the fledglings to
give them protection. Jesus likewise saw himself as a bird
brooding over his people. In response to the terrorism against
the Romans that was disrupting his land, he saw his role as a
peaceful "hen gathering her chicks."[5]

Two parables joined together in Luke 15 compare God to a
solicitous woman and a forgiving father in search of what they
have lost. The larger context of these parables adds significance
to this balancing of female and male images. An episode
recorded earlier in Luke's Gospel tells of "a woman of the city
who was a sinner"[6] entering the home where Jesus was dining
with a Pharisee named Simon. Jesus disgusted his host by ac-
cepting affection from this woman of ill-repute and by expressing forgiveness toward her. Luke introduces parables on a lost
and found theme by stating that the Pharisees had made this

complaint against Jesus: "This man welcomes sinners and eats with them." Jesus showed that his kindness toward disreputable persons of either gender was in accord with his theology. The God of Jesus was neither all masculine nor all feminine but embraced and transcended alleged gender characteristics. His outlook in this regard was quite different from the Pharisees' general outlook on women. Historian Josephus, who belonged to the Pharisaic party during that same century, expresses one thrust of Pharisees' scorn: "In every respect a woman is inferior to a man."[7]

According to a fragment of the lost Gospel of the Hebrews, Jesus referred to the Holy Spirit as "my mother."[8] This metaphor would have been obvious in the Jewish culture because the Hebrew word for Spirit (*ruah*) is feminine. She is often described as a life-giver in the Hebrew Bible. Job, for example, says, "The Spirit of God made me and gave me life."[9] The Odes of Solomon, the earliest Christian hymnbook, follows Jesus' Aramaic mother-tongue and refers to the Spirit as feminine. Recorded there is this figure: "The Holy Spirit opened her bosom. . . . I rested on the Spirit of Yahweh and she lifted me up to heaven."[10]

The Gospel of Philip in the third century echoes the Jewish tradition of understanding the Spirit to be female. On the assumption that the Spirit is "mother of many,"[11] the writer of this Gnostic Gospel argues against the notion of a virginal conception of Jesus: "Some say Mary was impregnated by the Holy Spirit. They err. They do not know what they say. When did a woman become pregnant by a woman?"[12] On the basis of Isaiah's comparison of Yahweh to a mother comforting her child and Jesus' reference to "the Comforter, the Holy Spirit,"[13] an early Syrian theologian named Makarios concludes that "the Spirit is our mother."[14]

It is evident, therefore, that Jesus did not think of God in exclusively male images. His references to God as *abba* — "Daddy" in his Aramaic tongue — was to stress the closeness of the divine-human bond, not to emphasize masculinity in the

Creator. Jesus' God was more like a compassionate parent than like a stern judge or a remote monarch. His perception was like that of the psalmist who wrote: "As kind as a father is to his children, so kind is Yahweh to those who honor him."[15]

Why has it been so difficult to follow the lead of the Bible with respect to the language we use in reference to God? With some hyperbole Letha Scanzoni and Nancy Hardesty express the prevailing situation in most churches: "Any pastor who began by praying, 'Our Mother, who art in heaven . . . ' would probably be defrocked forthwith. Yet the Bible is not afraid to use that image of God."[16]

A shift of gender in Western culture with reference to the Holy Spirit illustrates the way masculinity has been absolutized in the god-talk of European languages. The Spirit first became masculinized when the Bible was translated into Latin, a language that was destined to have a heavy impact on the intellectual conceptualizing of the modern world. The feminine *ruah*, the most frequent term for "Spirit" in the Bible, was translated by *spiritus*, a masculine word in Latin. Augustine, the most influential of all Latin bishops, rejected as "absurd" the gynomorphic imagery for the Holy Spirit which he found in Greek Christianity. Due perhaps to his own guilt-filled memories of illicit coitus, he was "offended" by efforts to associate the Holy Spirit with the feminine. Augustine claimed such imagery "offend us in carnal things, because we think of bodily conceptions and births."[17]

From Augustine's era onward maternal symbols of God have been suppressed and andromorphic imagery has been used almost exclusively. In churches that developed from Latin Christianity, the masculine pronoun is consistently used in reference to the Holy Spirit. For example, a paragraph on the "gifts of the Spirit" in a document of the Vatican II Council contains these pronouns: "He summons . . . he frees."[18] An example from Protestantism can be found in the basic doctrine of the Presbyterian Church. In a brief section describing the Holy Spirit, the masculine pronoun is used ten times in such sentences as: "He is the Lord and Giver of life. . . . He regenerates men by his grace."19

Even though the worship of a male, or androlatry (to coin a word), has been prominent in Western civilization, it was not a part of biblical culture. God was occasionally conceived of as a comforting mother, or as a companionate wife, or as a philosophical woman. Accordingly, those who claim to be made in the image of the God of the Bible are increasingly using female as well as male metaphors to express their devotional, artistic, and theological convictions.

THE GOSPEL AND WO/MAN

Jesus carried forward the concern for dignifying the role of woman articulated in the Genesis creation stories. He did far more than any other biblical personality to put into practice the affirmation that females and males share the image of God. How did he raise the status of women?

Rejecting the double standard in sexual morality was one way by which Jesus witnessed to all men and women being created equal. Typical of most societies, a woman in his culture received harsher treatment for sexual infidelity than a man. To frighten a confession out of a woman accused of becoming pregnant by someone other than her husband, she was dressed in black and brought to the eastern gate of the Jerusalem temple. There a priest humiliated her by untying her hair and tearing her dress so that her bosom was publicly exposed.20 Then he required her to drink a mixture of holy water, dust from the sanctuary, and ink from the scroll on which the accusation against her was written. Guilt is certain if the potion causes a miscarriage and "her face turns yellow and her eyes bulge and her veins swell."21 If she suffers no physical damage from that terrifying psychological ordeal, her innocence is presumed to have protected her.

In contrast to that "bitter water" test administered to half-naked women by pitiless priests, Jesus believed it was unjust to treat punitively only one partner in a liaison. Thus when some men alleged that a couple had been detected in "the very act of adultery," he was indignant that the Pharisees brought only the woman before him. To these zealots Jesus said, "Let him who is without sin among you be the first to throw a stone at her."[22] He dealt sternly with the self-righteous male accusers and gently with the adulterous woman—although he did not condone her behavior.

There are several other subtle but telling ways in which Jesus subverted the antifeminism of his day. First, he avoided the chronic male proclivity toward stereotyping women. There is no instance of Jesus cautioning men about the wiles of women. Rather, he viewed all humans as individuals, without classifying behavior as masculine or feminine. Second, Jesus had no reluctance to draw examples in his teaching from situations involving either sex. Parables with a primary focus on women—the ten bridesmaids, the leaven, the lost coin, and the unjust judge[23]—show that he empathized with various situations faced by women. He commended the generosity of a woman and a man.[24] Third, Jesus attempted to counteract economic discrimination against women. He was angered by those who pretend to be faithful Jews while they "devour widows' houses."[25] Fourth, he helped numerous women as well as men regain physical and moral health.

Both male and female interpreters have been impressed by Jesus' sexual egalitarianism. Harry E. Fosdick, for example, provides this apt description of Jesus' outlook on women: "He treated women as he treated men—as persons sacred in their own right, as souls loved of God and full of undisclosed possibilities. He never condescended to women, but habitually showed them deference, and to the surprise of the attendant audience more than once came to their spirited defense."[26] Dorothy Sayers thinks that women were especially drawn to Jesus because he treated them with dignity:

> They had never known a man like this man . . . who took their questions and arguments seriously; who never

mapped out their sphere for them, never urged them to be feminine or jeered at them for being female. . . . There is no act, no sermon, no parable in the whole Gospel that borrows its pungency from female perversity; nobody could possibly guess from the words and deeds of Jesus that there was anything "funny" about woman's nature.[27]

When questioned about his interpretation of the biblical doctrine of marriage, Jesus referred to the Eden creation story. Some Pharisees had asked: "Is it lawful to divorce one's wife for any cause?"[28] The point of the inquiry is contained in the phrase "for any cause." The Jews did not dispute the legality of divorce but the legitimate grounds for divorce. According to Deuteronomic law, a husband could divorce his wife if he found "some indecency" in her.[29] At issue was what made a woman indecent. In the first century before the Christian era, Shammai contended that "a man may not divorce his wife unless he has found unchastity in her." Hillel, another prominent rabbi, affirmed that a man had the right to divorce his wife for any cause — "even if she spoiled a dish for him."[30]

Divorce was exclusively a male prerogative in ancient Jewish culture. The Mishnah states that a wife can be "put away with her consent or without it."[31] No hearing was required before a court of justice. The disgruntled husband had only to hand her a *get* paper and tell her to get out! Yet a wife could not divorce her husband even if he were cruel and lecherous.

There is considerable evidence that Hillel's liberal interpretation of the divorce law was in line with past precedence. The oldest extant Jewish marriage contract indicates that in the fifth century B.C. a husband could capriciously divorce his wife without offering a reason, although reciprocal action by his wife was not sanctioned.[32] In the second century, divorce was advised on trivial grounds: "If your wife does not obey you at a signal or a glance, separate from her."[33] Philo — Jesus' contemporary — indicated that divorce was easy to procure.[34] Josephus spoke dispassionately of his many serial marriages and of divorcing those who "displeased him."[35] Rabbi Akiba believed that one should divorce and remarry "if he finds another woman more beautiful."[36]

Before Jesus began his ministry, Palestinian King Herod Antipas became enamored of his brother's wife Herodias. She agreed to abandon her husband and marry Antipas if he would forsake a wife who was the daughter of the Nabatean king, Aretas.[37] When Antipas agreed to this scheme — irregular even by the tolerant mores of the time — criticism arose in his kingdom. John the Baptist was beheaded because he condemned the scandal.[38]

Believing that the sanctity of marriage was being denigrated by the widespread flippant attitude toward divorce, Jesus declared what he held to be the Creator's reason for making two human sexes. Rather than citing the grounds for divorce championed by Shammai, Hillel, or Moses, he directed his interlocutors to the view of marriage recorded in Genesis 2. Thus he avoided becoming involved in legalism while pointing to the ideal of permanent monogamy. Significantly, Jesus considered the last word on marriage to be the first word in his Bible. He appealed to the Yahwist account which stresses the companionship reason for marriage. This distinguishes it from the later Priestly account which focuses on procreation. His quotation, "The two shall become one flesh," is the climax of an episode that begins with a criticism of the single state. Jesus' comments on matrimony in Eden display that he did not regard it as second best to the celibate condition. After pointing to the ideal of a prolonged two-in-one cleaving, Jesus states that the Torah permitted divorce because of "hardheartedness."[39]

By quoting a Genesis verse affirming that a couple become "one flesh," Jesus showed that he had no personal opinion that superseded the Genesis ideal. An understanding of Genesis 2:24 is increased by looking at the several facets of the Hebrew term *basar* ("flesh"). Unlike the later Hellenistic concept of flesh, there was no Hebraic dichotomy between the tainted flesh and the higher soul. For the Hebrews a human was not a spirit wearing a garment of flesh; rather, the total self was called flesh. Thus, in the Eden story "one flesh" basically means one's whole self. Other meanings of *basar* have subordinate bearing on this verse: the genitals, a kinship tie, and mortals in contrast to God.[40] By combining these varied meanings we find that this verse refers to a bond similar to that with blood relations. Moreover, "one flesh" connotes an intimate psychological interacting as well as a union of genital organs.

The New Testament concept of personal unity was not destructive to individuality. When Jesus advocated two-in-one matrimony and when he prayed in a Jerusalem upper room for his followers to "be one,"[41] he did not intend to reject personality differences among his disciples which he had heretofore encouraged. The composer of the Ephesian letter found a parallel between the Genesis 2 description of marriage and the ideal bonding pattern between Jesus and his followers.[42] In both marital and church relationships there should be a glad acceptance of differentiation. Rather than personal identity becoming extinguished, it is made more distinctive. The experience is one of mutual submission without absorption. Each participant becomes aware of ways in which his or her specialized roles enhance the whole corporate unity. Only after this awareness of individual differences is fully acknowledged and appreciated can an understanding of complementariness occur.

Jesus found the highest standard of sex and marriage in the prelegal order of creation. A tacit assumption here is that marriage should not be considered principally a legal contract involving dowry payments, clerical pronouncements, and registered certificates. Rather, the original and final norm for all humans, Jew and Gentile alike, is that marriage is an unconditional interpersonal covenant witnessed by God.[43] Thus the nuptial bond is essentially not one the social order can give or take away. Omitted from Jesus' view was the magical presumption of a later time that no marriage could be valid unless a certified representative of God or the state performed the proper ritual. He did not consider the remedy for the frivolous attitude toward divorce to be new judicial enactment or priestly benedictions at weddings. For him the marriage bond occurred when two were joined by God, whose quintessence is love; they were thereby committed to one another permanently. Jesus was convinced that self-righteous vindictiveness that scorns and abandons is a travesty of divine-human love. Consequently he unflaggingly emphasized divine forgiveness to the repentant.

Shakespeare's ode to "the marriage of true minds" expresses Jesus' comprehension of love in an exquisite manner:

> Love is not love
> Which alters when it alteration finds
> Or bends with the remover to remove.
> O no! It is an ever-fixed mark
> That looks on tempests and is never shaken. . . .
> Love's not time's fool, though rosy lips and cheeks
> Within his bending sickle's compass come.[44]

Jesus appealed to what George F. Moore calls the "utopian element" of Jewish ethical teaching.[45] In this and other situations he viewed the conduct of life not in terms of legal requirements, but in terms of fulfilling the categorical moral imperative of love. For those who see the meaning of life from that vantage point, questions about grounds for divorce become trivial and banal. "What God has joined" was Jesus' way of referring to his marital idealism. Like some rabbis he endorsed the proverb: "Marriages are made in heaven." They believed that ever since creation "the Holy One has been sitting in heaven arranging marriages."[46] In Jewish tradition this providential claim is based on the statement in Genesis 24:50 concerning Isaac's marriage: "The thing proceeds from Yahweh."[47]

THE MALE / FEMALE ROLE MODEL

Mythology, attitudes, and behavior are interrelated in a complex manner. Often behavioral changes cause attitudinal changes and these result in new conceptions of divine-human relationships. However, an opposite causal sequence sometimes accounts for changes in outlook and practice. What follows is an exploration of the way in which Jesus' thought and conduct reflected his androgynous theology. Presuming that Jesus shared the self-awareness that some early Christians had of him, namely that he was "the image of the invisible God,"[48] then it follows that he reflected the concept of deity declared in Genesis 1. The distinctiveness of his life-style will be displayed by comparing it with the prevailing outlook of most world cultures.

Men have always enjoyed putting women in their "place." From ancient times onward, men have made sharp contrasts between the alleged traits of the sexes. In Chinese culture the masculinity principle, *yang*, has been associated with steadfastness and brightness; *yin*, the femininity principle, has denoted softness and passivity. In Western civilization, the Pythagoreans exalted rationality and rectitude by calling them masculine qualities; they expressed disdain for the irrational and crooked by labeling them feminine qualities.[49] Euripides depicted women in one drama as having an inborn bent toward jealousy and in another drama they are portrayed as gossips by nature.[50] Jewish philosopher Philo wrote: "Man is informed by reason; woman by sensuality."[51]

An androcentric classification of character traits still abounds in this century in scholarly as well as in popular writings. For example, Sigmund Freud declared that women by nature are more prone than men to behave in egocentric, jealous, and unjust ways.[52] In a somewhat milder tone, psychiatrist Erich Fromm asserted that the preponderance of such qualities as thought and discipline in men is balanced by the concentration of receptiveness and endurance in women.[53] Theologian Emil Brunner wrote:

The biological sexual function in the man and the woman
has its exact counterpart in the mental and spiritual nature
of both sexes. . . . The man inclines to be objective, the
woman to be subjective; the man seeks the new, the
woman preserves the old. . . . He has less difficulty than
the woman in admitting that he is a sinner. . . . She is far
more sexual than the man.[54]

The life of Jesus illustrates the artificiality of these polariza-
tions of human characteristics. It is significant that the Gospel
writers describe the superlative model of Christian morality as
having traits that traditionally have been at least as much associated with females as with males. To show that this is the
case, an examination will be made of several.

The tender emotions have customarily been associated with
women. For example, philosopher Arthur Schopenhauer
believed that "women show more sympathy for the unfortunate
than men."[55] In the Gospels, however, Jesus is especially noted
for his sympathetic ministry. The verb "to have compassion" —
the customary translation of a Greek term meaning "to be
moved in one's viscera" — is used in the New Testament exclusively with respect to Jesus' teaching and life. It refers to the
good Samaritan, to the father of the prodigal, and to the yearn-
ings of Jesus in response to those who desired to be taught, fed,
or healed.[56] Unlike Julius Caesar, who a century earlier had
announced triumphantly, "I came, I saw, I conquered," Luke
reports that Jesus *came* to Nain, *saw* a widow mourning over
the corpse of her only son, and *had compassion* on her.[57]

Weeping, a particular expression of the tender feelings, is
also primarily associated in Western civilization with the
female sex. Aristotle held that "woman is more compassionate
than man and more easily moved to tears."[58] In Shakespeare's
dramas, "to play the woman" means to weep.[59] By contrast, in
the biblical culture, weeping was associated as much with one
sex as with the other. Samson's infamous bride, for instance,
used her flow of tears to overcome her strong husband.[60] A
dame, like a dam, was associated with hydraulic force. But

weeping was also frequently a trait of the patriarchs and other male leaders.[61] Jeremiah, the most profuse weeper in the Bible, expressed himself in this poignant way: "Would that my head were all water, my eyes a fountain of tears; that I might weep day and night for my people's dead!"[62] The grief response of another prophet is summed up in the shortest biblical verse: "Jesus wept."[63] A New Testament letter claims that he "offered up prayers and petitions, with loud cries and tears."[64] Jesus was emotionally a true "son of David" for there are eight occasions recorded when the Judean David wept aloud.[65]

Devotion to children is another trait our society calls feminine. Martin Luther, for example, believed that anatomy determines function: "Women ought to stay at home; the way they were created indicates this, for they have broad hips and a wide fundament to sit upon, keep house and bear and raise children."[66] However, youngsters were a prominent concern of Jesus even though he probably lacked the pear shape which Luther thought best equipped those with that special interest. Consider the simile Jesus used in his lament over Jerusalem. Alarmed by violence directed toward the innocent in his nation, Jesus pictured his role as a sheltering mother: "How often have I longed to gather your children around me as a hen gathers her brood under her wings, but you would not let me!"[67] He was no strutting and fighting cock! Jesus also identified with children by announcing that cordiality to them was a way of receiving him.[68] When the priests were indignant over his permitting children to shout hosannas, he reminded them of their Scriptures: "Have you never read that text, 'Thou hast made the lips of children and infants vocal with praise'?"[69]

Lord Chesterfield disparagingly asserted that women remain children throughout life.[70] But Jesus advised adults of either sex to "become like children," and he defined true greatness as keeping alive the virtues prominent in the very young.[71] Qualities he may have had in mind are trustfulness, frankness, forgiveness, and tolerance. Practicing what he preached, he recited on the cross a prayer of trust that Jewish children learned to say prior to going to sleep at night.[72]

Jesus shared with women the trait of gentleness. To the weary he said: "Come to me, all of you who are tired from carrying heavy loads, and I will give you rest. Take my yoke and put it on you, and learn from me, because I am gentle and humble in spirit."[73] Jesus' dealing with the adulterous woman is an example of his gentle approach to human relationships. He averted capital punishment for her and sends her off without condemnation.[74] Paul appealed to "the gentleness and kindness of Christ" in writing to the Corinthians.[75]

Salvador Dali wanted to capture Jesus' personal warmth in his Last Supper masterpiece. To accomplish this he used his wife to pose for the head of Jesus. Consequently the face is beardless and has a somewhat feminine appearance.

Submissiveness has also been deemed a feminine characteristic. As Mary Davies puts it:

> Women are door-mats and have been—
> The years those mats applaud—
> They keep their men from going in
> With muddy feet to God.[76]

Jesus stated that his mission in life was "not to be waited on but to wait on others," and he illustrated his humble role by washing his disciples' feet.[77] The washing of men's feet is referred to in the Bible as the function of handmaidens.[78]

Serving needy people in responsibilities beyond the home has also been a role more associated with women than with men. Among the qualities that composed an ancient Hebrew's picture of an ideal woman was this: "She is open-handed to the wretched and generous to the poor."[79] Today it is still the case that there is a high ratio of women in the areas of social work and nursing. Regarding Jesus' activity, this summary statement is given: "He went about doing good and healing all who were oppressed."[80] Assisting the social outcasts—prostitutes, beggars, lepers, and the like—was a main thrust of his mission.

Suffering is another trait especially associated with women. Before the coming of modern medicine with its painkillers, excruciating suffering was one of the dreads of childbirth. In the Hebrew creation story, the woman is told she will have intense parturient pains.[81] Inspired by the suffering servant ideal of Isaiah, Jesus said, "The Son of Man must undergo great sufferings."[82] Jesus exemplifies par excellence the traits of suffering and serving which traditionally have been more associated with females than with males. Also, he warned his followers that they will have to suffer like a woman in labor.[83]

Alfred Garvie has this to say about the "womanliness" of Jesus:

> His tenderness, gentleness, patience, and forbearance are more distinctly feminine than masculine graces. In his resignation and obedience to his Father's will, is there not a womanly rather than a manly submissiveness? The prominence he gives in the Beatitudes to the passive graces of endurance rather than the active virtues of endeavor vindicates the distinctive excellence of womanhood. His teaching about non-resistance, so much misunderstood and neglected, can be better appreciated by women than by men. . . . The mind of Jesus was intuitive rather than ratiocinative; his moral judgment was swift and sure; his spiritual discernment direct; and these are characteristics of women rather than of men.[84]

Those traits commonly thought to be masculine will now be sketched in relation to Jesus' personality. Aristotle claimed that men by nature are more dominant, courageous, persevering, and rational than women.[85] Those stereotypes have been transmitted rather uncritically down through our civilization until the present day. "Bold, resolute, and open in conduct" is the definition that Webster gives for "manly."

Jesus was noted for his leadership, fearlessness, powerfulness, and wisdom. Many were attracted to him by his charisma; some even left work, possessions, and home to follow him.[86]

On encountering a storm at sea that frightened even seasoned fishermen, Jesus was not worried.[87] His calmness in that situation resulted from keeping his power under control.

The power within Jesus was physical as well as spiritual. For most of his adult life he was in a manual trade which required bodily strength. Since there were no power tools for sawing and drilling, his muscles were likely even more developed than those of carpenters today. When he became an itinerant teacher, he warned those who joined his band that stamina was needed for coping with hardships greater than wildlife encounter.[88] Like a scoutmaster, he took his disciples on a long hike into the high Lebanese mountains.[89]

Jesus' assertiveness is expressed in his frequent denunciations of insincerity within the religious establishment. Here is a sample of one outburst of his anger: "The scribes and the Pharisees . . . don't practice what they preach. . . . They do all their deeds to be seen by men. . . . You blind guides, straining out a gnat and swallowing a camel! . . . Woe to you, scribes and Pharisees, hypocrites! for you are like whitewashed tombs, which outwardly appear beautiful, but within they are full of dead men's bones and every kind of corruption. . . . You brood of vipers!."[90] Then, at the risk of his life, he combined verbal criticism with physical force and drove out those who were using the Jerusalem temple as a marketplace.[91]

Mexican artist Jose Orozco may have been reflecting on the militant Jesus in the temple when he painted the mural now lodged at Dartmouth College. He presents a fierce but triumphant Jesus who has chopped down his cross and shattered the column of a building which represents the established order.

Self-confidence is associated more with males than with females. Jesus displayed assuredness in a superlative manner when he was on trial for his life. In an encounter with Roman governor Pilate, he was asked if he thought of himself as a Jewish king. Jesus replied: "I am a king. For this I was born, and for this I have come into the world, to bear witness to the truth; and all who are on the side of truth listen to me." Pilate remarked: "Surely you know I have power to release you or to have you crucified." To this Jesus asserted: "You would have no power over me unless it had been given you from above."[92]

In the masculine mystique of ancient Judaism it was assumed that reasoning was principally possessed by males and that no woman had the ability to acquire scholarly knowledge. It was thus in accord with sex role expectations for rabbi Jesus to have an intellectual command of his religious traditions and an ability to communicate fresh insights from that heritage.[93] The keenness of his mind is well illustrated in his handling of criticisms after driving out the temple moneychangers and animal sellers. Inquiries by the chief priests were made of Jesus with the purpose of embarrassing him regardless of his answer. Jesus cleverly responded to one loaded question about John the Baptist's authority by throwing back another question, one which his adversaries refused to answer. He then dealt astutely with a question involving giving to Caesar versus God by replacing the either/or dilemma with a both/and logic. According to Luke's Gospel, the Jerusalem leaders conceded that Jesus won this battle of wits: "They were unable to catch him in anything he had to say in public; they were amazed at his answer and were silenced."[94]

In this survey of some of Jesus' traits, it can be seen that he was liberated from the pernicious androcentrism of human history. As Elisabeth Moltmann-Wendel rightly observes: "He had himself personally integrated so many male and female behavioral characteristics that one could consider him the first maturely integrated person."[95] Rosemary Ruether expresses a similar assessment:

> Jesus is not so much "feminine" or "masculine" as he is a figure that defies all such sex stereotyping. Although authoritative, he is authoritative in an iconoclastic way. "He speaks with authority, not as the scribes and the Pharisees." His is an authority that overthrows conventional models of patriarchal, hierarchal, religious and political power systems; that champions women, the poor,

the unwashed and outcasts, that rejects the power games
of the male leadership classes.[96]

Thus qualities that many cultures have considered feminine
or masculine were harmoniously blended in his life-style. Jesus
was both a brave, brainy, and brawny he-man and a sensitive,
submissive, and suffering she-man! He affectionately took
children in his arms, but he also indignantly took strong-arm
methods to drive out temple hucksters. He surprised his com-
panions by being both more "feminine" and more "masculine"
than others.

Jesus' gender is not emphasized in the Greek New Testament. He is referred to as male (*aner*, or *andros*, genitive) only
several times,[97] but he is frequently called *anthropos* (human
being). Paul, the first New Testament author, refers to Jesus
only as *anthropos*. The founder of Christianity is described to
the Philippians as one who "appeared among us as *anthropos*
and became humbly obedient to death by crucifixion."[98] In the
Romans letter, Paul contrasts the sinful *adam* with the last
adam, claiming that the effect of the latter is vastly greater.
Christians receive God's gift "in the grace of the one *anthropos*,
Jesus Christ."[99] Paul did not view Jesus as primarily a male but
as the generic man who defines for females and males what it
genuinely means to be fully human.

In the Fourth Gospel, Jesus' admirers as well as his adversaries designate him by the term which includes women as well
as men. "No *anthropos* ever spoke like this *anthropos*!" exclaim
some temple guards.[100] "Behold the *anthropos*!" heralded Pilate.[101] The inclusive term for gender becomes a self-designa-
tion when Jesus comments to some opponents: "You seek to
kill me, an *anthropos* who has told you the truth."[102]

The creeds of the first ecumenical councils held at Nicea and
at Chalcedon use *anthropos* several times to describe Jesus' man-
hood. Ironically, in spite of this treatment of gender in the Greek
New Testament and in the early Greek creeds, the idea developed
in the Greek Orthodox Church that Jesus expresses perfect masculinity while his mother expresses perfect femininity.[103]

Sarah Grimke, an early modern feminist, observed that the Bible does not advise women to be soft and men stern. Rather, "both are equally commanded to bring forth the fruits of the Spirit: love, meekness, gentleness, etc."[104] She was alluding to the Galatian letter, where Paul also stated that "there is neither male nor female, for you are all one in Christ Jesus." The apostle was, of course, not unmindful of the physical differences between the sexes. He was, at least in that letter, recognizing a moral equality between the sexes and the qualities they should jointly share. Elsewhere he exhorted Christians to "put on compassion, kindness, humility, gentleness, patience,"[105] a cluster of excellences commonly associated in our culture with femininity at its best.

A judgment of Theodore Roszak is in line with Paul's assessment:

There are no masculine and feminine virtues. There are only human virtues. Courage, daring, decisiveness, resourcefulness are good qualities, in women as in men. So, too, are charity, mercy, tenderness. But ruthlessness, callousness, power, lust, domineering self-assertion . . . are destructive, whether in man or woman.[106]

Those who regard the imitation of Christ as normative should have no anxiety over whether or not they fit into what culture artificially calls "masculine" or "feminine" roles. They can internalize the best of the traditional values associated with the opposite sex without being less a member of their own sex. In particular, Jesus sets the male at liberty to express his temperament and talents even though some may ridicule as effeminate his tears, needlework, or the like. For example, in the 1972 presidential campaign, Senator Edmund Muskie choked back tears in public over a published false charge pertaining to his wife. Many Americans, who evidently think a male candidate should be unflappable, were appalled by his honest expression of tender feelings and thought it would be dangerous to entrust our highest office to a man who was so unstable as to weep. It was reported that "the moment of weakness left many voters wondering about Muskie's ability to stand up under stress."[107] Our nation preferred the tough politician who began his career by denouncing those who were "soft on communism" and who as president expressed his machismo by bombing Hanoi remorselessly. President Nixon ended his career by fighting dauntlessly to clear his name from scandal. Writing in the wake of our Vietnam debacle, Carolyn Heilbrun warns: "So long as we continue to believe the 'feminine' qualities of gentleness, lovingness and the counting of cost in human rather than nation or property terms are out of place among rulers, we can look forward to continued self-brutalization and perhaps even to self-destruction."[108]

Sexist outlooks, which are based on culture rather than creation, should be rejected. But the alternative need not be a unisex sameness that thwarts the maximizing of individual variations. Rather, the liberated male and female have heightened options for temperamental expressions. Like Jesus, they can choose from a broad arc of possible human traits and reunite what culture has split asunder. Into their personalities they can combine — as Jesus did — qualities as varied as shedding tears with impunity over the plight of our nation's capital on one day, and striking forcefully against corrupt business practice on the next. Jesus was a revolutionary but his sphere was more psychological than political. He worked to free individuals from gender polarization that continues to be severely constricting.

Chapter 6

Paradise Continued

"Paradise" is a loanword from the Persians for describing a lovely enclosed park. The famed Persian Omar Khayyam conveys its sensuousness in this exquisite poem:

> A Book of Verses underneath the Bough,
> A Jug of Wine, a loaf of Bread — and Thou
> Beside me singing in the Wilderness —
> Oh, Wilderness were Paradise now![1]

The first translators of Genesis borrowed *pardes* to express to the Mediterranean cultures what the Garden of Eden symbolized. For the Hebrews it connoted the ideal environment where harmony reigned among the Creator, humans, and animals. *Pardes* is also used in a highly figurative passage of the Song of Songs to refer to a natural setting conducive to lovemaking. The bridegroom describes the honeymoon experience in this manner:

> Your lips distil nectar, my bride;
> Honey and milk are under your tongue. . . .
> Your shoots [nipples?] are a *pardes* of
>   pomegranates.[2]

Many wrongly think in a temporal and spatial mode when they use the term *paradise*. Some imagine it to refer to an idyllic place that existed prior to the advent of evil. For Rousseau and Marx, paradise was the primeval condition before the institution of private property. Some presume it refers to the remote future when peace between God and creation will finally triumph. In Jewish eschatology, paradise was a heavenly banquet where the reassembled bodies of the righteous would join with Enoch and others who "walk with God." But *pardes* as used in the Jewish Bible describes God's continual creation. It has a contemporaneity unrelated to geography or chronology, so it is no-where and no-when.

THE GENESIS UTOPIA

What ingredients of the Hebrew conception of paradise are contained in the opening chapter of Genesis? Having a cosmic orientation, this myth by the Priestly composer deals with the question, what is the main purpose of the components of the vast universe? The answer: celestial bodies, oceans, and organic life show the *tov* of the Almighty Creator. *Tov*, repeated throughout the chapter, is a term with both an esthetic and moral connotation. Everything was created to show the beauty as well as the goodness of God—especially men and women who bear the divine likeness. Responsibility for filling and controlling the paradisiacal earth is assigned to humans. Along with other animals, humans are given a vegetarian diet. "The lion shall eat grass like the ox"[3] was Isaiah's rendering of the tranquil utopia.

A separate creation myth found in Genesis 2 focuses on a terrestrial paradise. The Yahwist composer is not interested in astronomy, or even in the seas and its fishes. The story rather deals with the question, what are the purposes of human creation? Hence the human is first in the sequence of created things, a compound of potter's clay and divinity. After Yahweh causes the desert to bloom, the inspired dust is placed in an oasis filled with visual and palatal delights. This perennially verdant garden is at the headwaters of the earth's rivers. The human works as a caretaker to keep the flora continually productive and beautiful. Thus, the Yahwist mythmaker affirms that the first purpose of human creation is to enjoy and preserve nature.

The second purpose of creation is associated with "the tree of the knowledge of good and evil." This Hebrew expression is difficult to translate, but it refers to omniscience — a quality presumed to be an attribute of God alone. The human is confronted with a simple choice for demonstrating responsibility. The consequences of the exercise of moral freedom are awesome: if obedient to God and humble in assumptions about the attainment of knowledge, the fruit of "the tree of life" — representing everlasting life — will be given; if disobedient and hubristic, spiritual death will ensue.

Companionship is the third purpose of human creation. Various animals are created as potential partners, but the human rejects zoophilia. Although the story does not indicate why there is a discontinuity between humans and other animals, sexual behavior is one significant difference. Animal rutting is primarily for venereal relief and a female receives a male only when in heat. In most species these infrequent physiological encounters are largely devoid of individual affection. Because of this and other incompatibilities, Yahweh acts as a surgeon to effect a partner who is truly fit. The human is divided and two sexes are fashioned from the separate parts. This second experiment is successful because an urge for intimate companionship arises. The incomplete person breaks out in a love song: "This one at last is bone of my bone and flesh of my flesh!"

The bond between the two is so strong that parental ties become secondary. After leaving father and mother, the man "cleaves to his wife and they become one flesh." Amazingly, this marriage is unconstrained by the ancient conventions of patriarchy which involved the bride — but not the groom — leaving the parental home. The wedding in Paradise concludes with the comment: "They were both naked but unashamed."

Samuel Terrien contrasts this Genesis 2 story with subsequent views of sexuality in the Judeo-Christian culture:

> The myth breathes an atmosphere of unabashed sen-
> suality. There is no puritanical or ascetic disparagement
> of sexuality. The story contains not the slightest hint of
> moral or cultic impurity. There is the distinct absence of
> any statement concerning legal uncleanliness of genital
> secretions, sexual abstinence at sacred times or during
> menstruation, need for ritual cleansing, or moral atoning
> or purification for an act considered as ritually impure or
> sinful. The coming together of the couple is the healthy
> fulfilling of the Creator's intention, without shadow or
> qualification.[4]

THE SONG OF SONGS

Around 500 B.C., when some Hebrews were devising leviti-
cal legislation aimed at depreciating sexual functions, some
love poems were composed and then preserved with a title in-
dicating excellence. "Song of songs," like "king of kings," was
the Hebrew idiom for expressing superlative degree. Desig-
nated as the loveliest Hebrew song, it shows that some within
Israel retained the outlook of the composer of the Eden creation myth.

The Song can be viewed as a midrash or commentary on the
concluding portion of Genesis 2, especially expanding on the
verbs "cleave" and "unashamed." The Jewish midrash was an
imaginative interpretation which broadened and deepened a
portion of the Torah. Liberties were taken with the biblical text
in order to provide treatments that would be both entertaining
and morally edifying. Francis Landy argues that "the Song
transforms the images and motifs of the story of the Garden of
Eden, so that it can be seen as a commentary on it." Although
finding in the pastoral Song no conscious dependence, he
thinks both are preoccupied with a nostalgia for Paradise.[5]

How is the Song of Songs a continuation of those purposes of human creation found in Genesis? First, the Song describes the sensuous delights of the plants of Paradise:

> The fig tree puts forth its figs,
> And the vines are in blossom;
> They give forth fragrance.6

The Song also tells of other lush trees and the succulent fruit they produce.7 Moreover, the enjoyment of nature is associated with the aroma of these spices: henna, saffron, cinnamon, frankincense, myrrh, and aloes.8 The Song focuses on a couple who live mainly in the out-of-doors, where the wooded countryside forms the walls and roof of their dwelling:

> Our couch is green;
> The beams of our house are cedar,
> Our rafters are pine.9

The flora is nourished by mountain streams:

> A garden fountain, a spring of gushing water,
> Cascading down from Lebanon.10

The folk lyrics are especially sensitive to the way in which Palestinian springtime mirrors the awakening of love:

> Arise, my love, my fair one, and come away;
> For lo, the winter is past,
> The rain is over and gone.
> The flowers appear on the earth,
> The time of singing has come,
> And the cooing of the turtledove is heard in the
>   land.11

According to the Song, the marvelous environment is not

intended to be a place of endless, idle indulgence. Humans work in their particular marvelous settings to take care of domestic plants and animals. The woman is tanned by the sun while cultivating grapes. Both genders share the labor of pasturing flocks.[12]

A dominant motif of the Song is that humans are created for close companionship. Animals are frequently mentioned, but not as sharers in the social community—or even as pets. The Song refers to foxes, lions, leopards, and other wild animals, often because they provide picturesque analogies:

> Roam, my beloved, like a gazelle,
> Or a young stag upon spice mountains.[13]

Her lover responds, also using animal imagery:

> Your eyes are doves behind your veil,
> Your hair is like a flock of goats. . . .
> Your breasts are like two fawns.[14]

While finding animals lovely and useful, the Song does not speak of them as a cure for loneliness. When the pain of separation is described, it is evident that only a human companion of the opposite sex can relieve the agony. The bride tells of a dream in which she searched for her lost lover:

> When I found him whom I love
> I clung to him, and would not let him go
> Until I had brought him into my mother's house,
> And into the chamber of her that conceived me.[15]

The lyrics carry the common theme that fulfillment can be found in an intimate male-female relationship. The two "cleave" together with their naked bodies, not primarily to reproduce but to express their mutual love. The fact that procreation is not mentioned in the Song indicates that the bond between the lovers has an intrinsic value apart from breeding capabilities.

Both the Eden story and the Song romance have overtones of a wedding celebration. Some lines of the Song also suggest that the bridal couple engaged in some royal role-playing during the days of the festivities. The groom pretended to be a king and the bride a queen in accord with Near Eastern custom. In ancient Judaism crowns were worn at weddings,[16] probably in imitation of royalty. Since Solomon was the greatest lover in Israel — at least on a quantitative scale — some of the nuptial activity probably consisted in carrying the groom down the street in a palanquin resembling the luxurious Solomonic throne chair — fantasized to have silver posts, gold back, and purple seat. The wedding guests sang:

> Go forth . . . and behold King Solomon,
> Wearing the crown with which his mother crowned
>   him
> On the day of his wedding.[17]

The bride was honored by her maids as a Solomoness (the probable meaning of "Shulammite)."[18] This female counterpart of the solomonic bridegroom sings:

> My king has brought me into his chambers;
> We will rejoice together.[19]

The Song evokes both negative and positive memories of Solomon. The king was a notorious polygamist who possessed an enormous harem. This conflicts with the high value placed on pair-bonding in the Song, so Solomon is treated with ambivalence. "You, O Solomon, may have the thousand," may allude to his 700 wives and 300 concubines.[20] The Song's groom invidiously compares those queens and concubines to his unique bride. He boasts: "My dove, my perfect one, is only one."[21] Solomon and all his glory is not arrayed like his "lily of the valley."[22]

In the Song, as in Eden, the partnership is genuine. Nowhere in ancient literature can such rapturous mutuality be paralleled. The maiden initiates the erotic exchange:

Let me drink the kisses of your mouth;
For your caresses are better than wine.[23]

From that ardent opening onward, she more than holds her own in the recorded lines. She admires his radiant and ruddy complexion, his wavy raven-black hair, and his firm ivory-smooth body. His combination of strong muscles and delectable speech stimulates her desire.[24] The groom affectionately reciprocates by giving a toe-to-head description as she dances. Her feet are graceful, her thighs rounded, her breasts ripe, and her breath aromatic.[25] Thus, without subservience, each admires certain sexy qualities in the other.

Recent interpreters have noted the egalitarian quality of the Song. Michael Fox writes: "Each lover invites the other to come away, each goes out to find the other, each knows moments of hesitation, each desires the culmination of their love as intensely as the other."[26] In this regard Phyllis Trible appropriately compares the couples of Eden and the Song:

Female and male are born to mutuality and love. They are naked without shame; they are equal without duplication. They live in gardens where nature joins in celebrating their oneness. Animals remind these couples of their shared superiority in creation as well as of their affinity and responsibility for lesser creatures. Fruits pleasing to the eye and to the tongue are theirs to enjoy. Living waters replenish their gardens. . . . Neither couple fits the rhetoric of a male dominated culture. As equals they confront life and death.[27]

The last way in which the Song echoes the Genesis 2 affirmations on the purposes of human creation is in responsible choice-making. The Song was not intended as an expression of undisciplined sexuality. There is a note of moral commitment throughout the Song. The bride is proud of having been a strong "wall" in her youth and not an open "door."[28] She restricted her sexual freedom and did not let down her defenses until she found the man of her dreams. Caution is advised in a constant refrain: "Do not awaken passion before it is ready to stir."[29] The groom is proud that his bride has been "a garden locked, a fountain sealed."[30] He looks forward to an exclusive and permanent relationship in the private park, when the bride removes the "no trespassing" sign:

> Let my love enter his garden,
> And partake of its choicest fruits.[31]

This monogamous bonding is "till death do us part." In the final chapter of the Song, the theme of steadfast love leaps to a blaze:

> Stamp me as a seal upon your heart,
> As a seal upon your arm;
> For love is as strong as death,
> And passion is as unyielding as the grave.
> Its flashes are bolts of lightning,
> A holy flame.
> Raging rivers cannot quench love,
> Nor can floods drown it.[32]

In the Eden story, temptation was placed within the ideal environment to convey that there can be no paradise without individuals voluntarily acting on standards that maximize life. In the Song the couple witness that faithfulness to each other, not promiscuity, is the way to bring true love to fruition.

THE SEXUAL AND THE SACRED IN HISTORY

Ancient peoples would have found the meaning of the folk lyrics collected in the Song as transparently clear as we do today. Descriptions of erotic encounters are found in the oldest written records onward. The Sumerians told of love-making and they emphasized the woman's initiative.[33] The Babylonians continued the romantic theme.[34]

Love's old sweet song, as expressed in Egypt in the second millennium, is closely parallel to the Song of Songs.[35] Both lyrics tell of love-sickness and use analogies from nature in a similar way. This can be shown by a sampling from an anthology of those Egyptian love poems.

> When I kiss her with her lips opened,
>   ah, then I am drunk without beer! . . .
> O would that I were the one who washes her linen,
>   to rinse the perfumes which pervade her
>   garments! . . .
> Her neck is long, and her nipple is radiant,
>   and her hair is deep sapphire.
> Her arms surpass the brilliance of gold,
>   and her fingers are like lotus blossoms.
> Her buttocks curve down languidly from her trim
>   belly. . . .
> Yes, she has captivated my heart in her embrace![36]

In Greece sensuous love poetry was written by Sappho in the sixth century, in the same period as the Song of Songs anthology was being collected by the Jews. She compares love to flowering meadows; she tells of delightful perfumes and joyous singing at a wedding. Sappho, like the anonymous composers of the Song of Songs, accentuates a woman's perspective in love-making.[37] This may suggest that much of the Song was composed by women. If so, it would probably stand alone in the Hebrew Bible as the only book not exclusively of male authorship.

The popularity of the Song in ancient Judaism was in part due to some who viewed its lines as smutty. Akiba criticized youth who sang the Song in taverns in a vulgar manner. Regarding the Bible, that distinguished rabbi was of the opinion that "all the writings are holy, but the Song of Songs is the Holy of Holies."[38]

The Song expresses love sentiments similar to those found in other books that the Jews included in their corpus of holy books. For example, the passion of the couple in the Song who are "intoxicated with love" is echoed in this poem:

Have pleasure with the wife of your youth!
A loveable doe! A sweet little mountain goat!
May her breasts always intoxicate you!
May you ever find rapture in loving her![39]

This emphasis upon romance within marriage explains why the Talmud recommends marital intercourse as a way of beginning the holy Sabbath.[40]

Sexual asceticism developed in Christianity in the third century with the rise of monasticism. Interpreters from that time onward have generally been embarrassed over the plain meaning of the Song and have ardently desired to substitute an opposing message. Hippolytus, a Roman Christian, started the desexing process by alleging that the admiration expressed in the Song for the maiden's two breasts really meant that the Old Testament and the New Testament were glorious. Those who embrace what those Testaments teach about killing fleshly desires will be elevated to "the hill of frankincense" referred to in the Song. Elsewhere I have described the bizarre way in which the celibate clergy used allegory in a conspiracy to remove concupiscence or sexual passion from human relationships.[41]

In the early Middle Ages the erotic in literature was so heavily suppressed that some European scholars have mistakenly presumed that erotic literature was not a part of pre-European civilizations. Denis de Rougemont, in his famous historical study of love, displayed little awareness of ancient social history when he claimed that romantic love began with feudalism.[42] Friedrich Engels also wrongly held that "the first historical form of sexlove as a passion" came in the age of chivalry.[43] However, as has been illustrated, romance had an important place in ancient cultures. Bards praised it as sweeter than honey and commended it for producing bonds stronger than a lion.

During the past half-century, religious people have been sweeping aside falsifying allegories and have been regaining appreciation for the original meaning of the Song of Songs. Two men who experienced Nazi imprisonment illustrate well the way in which the authentic meaning of the Song is inspiring people in our era. Lutheran pastor Dietrich Bonhoeffer contemplated its erotic lines when he was engaged to be married. Although gallows rather than marriage lay ahead, he makes this grand affirmation in a letter:

> God wants us to love him eternally with our whole hearts — not in such a way as to injure or weaken our earthly love. . . . Even in the Bible we have the Song of Songs; and really one can imagine no more ardent, passionate, sensual love than is portrayed there (see 7:6). It's a good thing that the book is in the Bible, in face of all whose who believe that the restraint of passion is Christian.[44]

When Jewish psychiatrist Viktor Frankl was separated from his wife in a concentration camp he was comforted by sentiments from the Song. His wife was executed but he survived and wrote about values he had discovered. One of the few scriptural quotations in *Man's Search for Meaning* is "love is as strong as death." He found that commitment to personal loyalty basic not only for marital relations but for all human relationships. "Love is the ultimate and the highest goal to which man can aspire," he concluded.[45] Frankl's perspective has had a wide impact because his idealism was nurtured while experiencing at close range history's worst expression of human depersonalization and butchery. He is critical of Freud's emphasis on alienating forces in the self that produce chaos in families and nations. Rather than stressing that humans are being pushed downward by their unconscious drives, Frankl focuses on showing that we can be pulled upward by the goals we choose.

Although biblical writers, from the Yahwist onward, are fully aware of human alienation, they are convinced that humans can ally themselves with forces more powerful than Eden's serpent. Genesis 3 onward tells of male domination, slavery, and other expressions of hostility in human relationships. The composers of the lyrics in the Song were also probably realistic enough to know that life is no continuous honeymoon. Recognizing the fragile status of Paradise, they nevertheless suggest that humans can be better motivated by pointing to life's raptures than to its torments.

Some churchleaders, shifting from an Augustinian obsession with original sin, human depravity, and the serpent, are beginning to accentuate original righteousness, creation goodness, and the turtledove. Karl Barth, a bellwether theologian during much of this century, found these latter themes to be therapeutic. Although often remembered for his analysis of the dark side of human nature at the time of Hitler, Barth wrote at length about the importance of the Song of Songs as a reaffirmation of Genesis 2.[46] He called Genesis 2 the first "Magna Charta of humanity" and the Song of Songs the second. This is the hope he finds in those declarations: "The beginning and end, the origin and goal, both between Yahweh and Israel and between man and woman, are as depicted in Genesis 2 and the Song of Songs. In retrospect of creation and prospect of the new creation of the last time, we can and may and must speak of man and woman as is done in these texts." Barth thinks the Song should be appreciated as erotic lyrics related to sealing the marriage covenant. It should not be transformed into a theological cryptogram, as has been the prevailing approach in the past, nor given the silent treatment, which is currently the approach of blushing Christians. Many clergy never preach a sermon on the Song, and church school literature generally disregards it.

Alan Watts observed that some Christian songs express praise for God's handiwork in nature, but sex is not mentioned. Had the hymn "For the Beauty of the Earth" followed the Song of Songs, he suggests, a stanza on the beauty of a woman's curvaceous breasts or a man's wavy locks would have been included. Watts boldly thinks that poets should have something to say about "the revelation of divine glory in the image of a naked girl, upon her marriage bed, squirming in bliss in the arms of her man."[47]

Stimulated by Watts's criticism, I have examined hymnbooks used by several denominations to see if his accusation is true. My analysis confirms that praise of sexuality is virtually nil. For example, "This is my Father's World," a favorite American hymn, acknowledges the wonders wrought by God in the skies, seas, rocks, plants, and birds. While affirming that God "shines in all that's fair," human affection is not explicitly mentioned. In a recently published British hymnbook I found a section entitled "Delight in Creation" which contained a dozen hymns. From the lyrics included in that section one would not guess that human sexuality was an important expression of divine activity in the natural world. Hopefully, hymnbook editors and composers of marriage manuals in the next century will have overcome their misplaced feelings of shame and will include lilting lines of sexual communion from Genesis 2 and from Israel's superlative Song.

German theologian Helmut Gollwitzer acknowledges his indebtedness to Barth in his recent *Song of Love*. Although not a composer of new hymns, Gollwitzer does illustrate an openness to sacramental sexuality that has been tragically absent during many centuries of church tradition. This is the way he sees the lovers in the Song of Songs:

How excited they are as each gazes at the full length of the other's naked body. . . . They are Adam and Eve in paradise, free of shame, in the happiness of sex. . . . Look at how all their senses are brought into play — seeing, hearing, smelling, tasting, touching! . . . Nothing is so unlike the animals as human sexuality. . . . It is not limited to the specific genital activity of procreation but encompasses the entire person in an act of complete concentration in and attention to the sex partner. . . . Neither is fully human without the other. The love play of their bodies and their physical union is both symbol and actualization of their belonging to each other completely.[48]

There is wholesomeness in proclaiming the good news of nature's joys and telling of the *tov* of sexual relations within marriage. Many of today's secular songs deal, as always, with sexual desire, but they tell of falling out as much as falling in love. There is more about infidelity than about constancy. The message of the biblical Paradise is counter to the notion that love soon vanishes and is not for keeps. The Song of Songs is devoted to the unquenchable fire of true love. The obscenity of sexual exploitation and the anti-ecological outlook on creation can best be countered by exalting the potentiality of human sexuality and lauding the pleasures of responsible enjoyment of all the beauties of nature.

In conclusion, the opening chapters of Genesis are significant for a reason often overlooked or misunderstood in the history of biblical interpretation. Rather than probing them for scientific disclosures on earliest human history or to ground a theological doctrine of mankind's Fall, the myths can best be examined for profound insights into normative relationships between women and men, and between both genders and their Creator. Careful textual study of biblical literature reveals that the God of the Hebrews and of Jesus was neither masculine nor feminine, but embraced and transcended traits which cultures assign to one gender or the other. Those who look upon woman as an inferior "rib" are doubly in error since the

Hebrew text of the Eden story supports neither the "rib" translation nor the subordinate status of woman. Reaffirmed in the
Song of Songs and in the Gospel is this theme from the creation myths: what the sexes share in common is more fundamental than what differentiates them. A tragedy of Judaism,
Christianity, and Islam has been the failure during most of their
history to comprehend and live by the equality ideal expressed
in its authoritative early traditions. Bigoted male interpreters
have literally manhandled Scriptures in order to justify family
domination by husbands and fathers and church rule by males.

What we see may be located behind rather than in front of
our eyeballs. Impressions stored in the brain often make fresh
considerations difficult. From the Hellenistic era onward the
pagan Pandora myth has been in the minds of European men
as they have examined literature and life. Augustine, the most
influential theologian of Western Christianity, introduced a
doctrine of original sin that associates sex more with the sinful
than with the sacred and finds women more culpable than men
for evil. The Bishop of Hippo's monumental perversion of the
biblical view of sexuality has had a pernicious effect on culture.
From witch-hunts of the Middle Ages to the continuing ex-
clusion of women from high positions, sexism has been devas-
tating to harmony among humans.

Jesus was convinced that both men and women share the
image of God. Accordingly, he avoided gender stereotyping,
he rejected the double standard in sexual morality, and he
criticized male-controlled divorce proceedings. In line with the
Genesis and the Song of Songs treatments of Paradise, he affirmed these purposes of human creation: to interact with
beautiful nature, to exercise moral freedom, and to enjoy permanent companionship. Much needs to be done to express the
implications of this motif in hymns, teachings, and conduct.

Notes

INTRODUCTION

1. J. W. Fulbright, *Old Myths and New Realities* (New York: Random House, 1964).

2. 2 Peter 1:16; cf. 1 Tim. 1:4, 4:7; 2 Tim. 4:4; Titus 1:14 (Revised Standard Version, hereafter RSV).

3. W. T. Jones, *The Classical Mind* (New York: Harcourt, Brace & World, 1969), p 134.

4. Cornelius Loew, *Myth, Sacred History, and Philosophy* (New York: Harcourt, Brace & World, 1967), pp. 42-43.

5. Brevard Childs, *Myth and Reality in the Old Testament* (London: Studies in Biblical Theology, 1962), p. 74.

6. Theodor Gaster, *Myth, Legend, and Custom in the Old Testament* (Gloucester, Mass.: Peter Smith, 1981), Vol. 1, pp. 10, 15.

7. Hosea 11:9; Isa. 31:3 (RSV).

8. See William Phipps, "Darwin and Cambridge Natural Theology," *Bios* 54 (1983), p. 218.

CHAPTER 1: ANDROGYNY IN MYTHS

1. *USA Today*, December 19, 1986.

2. Eric Marshall and Stuart Hample, *Children's Letters to God* (New York, Pocket Books, 1966), no pagination.

3. *The Presbyterian Outlook*, October 7, 1985, p. 5.

4. *The Christian Century*, August 26, 1987, p. 712.

5. Northrop Frye, *The Great Code* (New York: Harcourt, Brace Jovanovich, 1983), p. 107.

6. Cf. Leonard Swidler, *Biblical Affirmations of Woman* (Philadelphia: Westminster, 1979), p. 35.

7. Walther Eichrodt, *Theology of the Old Testament* (Philadelphia: Westminster, 1961), p. 185.

8. 1 Kings 11:5, 33 (RSV).

9. Elizabeth Stanton, ed., *The Woman's Bible* (New York: European Pub. Co., 1895), pp. 14-15.

10. Matilda Gage, *The History of the Woman Suffrage Movement* (Rochester, 1881), Vol. 1, p. 796.

11. George Buttrick, ed., *The Interpreter's Bible* (Nashville: Abingdon–Cokesbury, 1952), Vol. I, p. 301.

12. Erich Segal, ed., *Euripides* (Englewood Cliffs, NJ: Prentice–Hall, 1968), p. 154.

13. Quoted in Peter Engel, "Androgynous Zones," *Harvard*, (January 1985), p. 25.

14. Hosea 2:7; 11:9 (RSV).

15. Isa. 54:5; 66:13 (Good News).

16. Isa. 42:13-14 (Good News).

17. Isa. 49:15.

18. Isa. 40:18-26; 44:7-20.

19. Deut. 4:15-16.

20. John Calvin, *Institutes*, 1, 11, 8.

21. John Calvin, *Commentary on the Isaiah* (Grand Rapids: Eerdmans, 1948), on Isa. 42:14 and 49:15.

22. Kilmer Myers, "Should Women be Ordained? No," *The Episcopalian*, (February 1972), p. 9.

23. Albert DuBois, "Why I am Against the Ordination of Women," *The Episcopalian*, (July 1972), p. 22.

24. Mary Hayter, *The New Eve in Christ* (Grand Rapids: Eerdmans, 1987), p. 31.

25. United Church Board for Homeland Ministries, *Human Sexuality* (New York, 1977), p. 33.

26. Hans Kung, *On Being a Christian* (Garden City, NY:

Doubleday, 1976), p. 310.

27.   Elisabeth Moltmann-Wendel and Jurgen Moltmann, *Humanity of God* (New York: Pilgrim, 1983), p. 89.

28.   Elizabeth Clark and Herbert Richardson, eds., *Women and Religion* (New York: Harper & Row, 1977), pp. 164-165.

29.   Mircea Eliade, *A History of Religious Ideas* (Chicago: Univ. of Chicago Press, 1978), Vol. I, p. 165; Mircea Eliade, *The Two and the One* (London: Harvill, 1965), pp. 78-124; Joseph Campbell, *The Masks of God: Primitive Mythology* (New York: Viking, 1959), p. 104.

30.   *Brihadaranyaka Upanishad* 1, 4.

31.   *Greater Bundahishn* 101, 2-5.

32.   Plato, *Symposium* 189-193.

33.   Gen. 2:7-25.

34.   Stanton, *The Woman's Bible*, p. 21; Gal. 3:28.

35.   Eliade, *The Two and the One*, p. 106.

36.   2 Clement 12.

37.   *Eruvin* 18a; *Berakhot* 61a.

38.   *Genesis Rabbah* 8, 1.

39.   Eliade, *The Two and the One*, pp. 104-105.

40.   George Tavard, *Woman in Christian Tradition* (Notre Dame: University Press, 1973), p. 6.

41.   Mark 10:8-9.

42.   Maisie Ward, *Return to Chesterton* (New York, 1952), p. 90.

43.   Margaret Mead, *Sex and Temperament in Three Primitive Societies* (New York: New American Library, 1950), p. 190.

44.   Paul Mussen, "Early Sex-Role Development" in David Goslin, ed., *Handbook of Socialization Theory and Research* (Chicago: Rand McNally, 1969), pp. 707-729.

45.   John Money and Anke Ehrhardt, *Man and Woman, Boy and Girl* (Baltimore: John Hopkins, 1972).

46.   Sandra Bem, "Androgyny versus the Tight Little Lives of Fluffy Women and Chesty Men," *Psychology Today*, September 1975), pp. 60-62.

47.   Abigail Stewart and Brinton Lykes, eds. *Gender and Personality* (Durham: Duke Univ. Press, 1985), p. 312.

CHAPTER 2: A BONE OF CONTENTION

1.   Andreas Vesalius, *De Humani Corporis Fabrica Libri Septem* (1543), 1, 19.

2.   *Genesis Rabbah* 18, 2.

3.   *Genesis Rabbah* 17, 8.

4.   Al-Baghawi, *Mishkat al-Masabih.*

5.   Augustine, *The Literal Meaning of Genesis* 11, 37, 50.

6.   Aquinas, *Summa Theologica* 1, q. 98, 2; Augustine, *De Genesi ad Litteram* 9, 5, 9.

7.   Aquinas, *Summa Theologica* 1, q. 92, 3.

8.   Aristotle, *The Generation of Animals* 737a 28.

9.   *Summa Theologica* 1, q. 92, 1.

10.   Heinrich Kramer and James Sprenger, *Malleus Maleficarum* (New York: Dover, 1971), p. 44.

11.   Joseph Swetnam, *The Araignment of Lewde, Idle, Froward, and Unconstant Women* (London, 1616), p. 1.

12.   *Erubim* 18a.

13.   Carroll Camden, *The Elizabethan Woman* (London: Elsevier Press, 1952), p. 25; Theodor Reik, *The Creation of Woman* (New York: McGraw Hill, 1960), p. 25.

14.   Thomas Moore, "The Rabbinical Origin of Women," *Poetic Works* (1826), Vol. IV.

15.   F. S. Boad, ed., *The Taming of a Shrew* (London: Chatto and Windus, 1908), pp. 62-63.

16.   Francis de Sales, *Introduction to the Devout Life* 3, 38.

17.   John Milton, *Paradise Lost* 4, 484 and 488.

18.   Ibid. 10, 149, 884, 888-894.

19.   C. L. Powell, ed., *The Works of John Milton* (New York: Columbia Univ. Press, 1931), Vol. IV, p. 93.

20.   Richard Whitlock, *Zootomia* (1654), p. 61.

21.   George Byron, *Don Juan* 11, 46.

22.   Elizabeth Stanton, ed. *The Woman's Bible* (New York: European Pub. Co., 1895), p. 7.

23.   James Frazer, *Folk-Lore in the Old Testament* (Lon-

don: Macmillan, 1918), Vol. I, p. 5.

24.   Eugene Bianchi and Rosemary Ruether, *From Machismo to Mutuality* (New York: Paulist Press, 1976), p. 12.

25.   Simone de Beauvoir, *The Second Sex* (New York: Knopf, 1957), p. 141; Paula Stern, "The Womanly Image," *The Atlantic Monthly*, (March 1970), p. 87; Kate Millett, *Sexual Politics* (New York: Doubleday, 1971), p. 80.

26.   *Sanhedrin* 39a.

27.   Quoted in Bede Jarrett, *Social Theories of the Middle Ages* (New York, 1966), p. 72.

28.   John Dryden, "Amphytrion," Prologue.

29.   William Austin, *Haec Homo* (London, 1637), pp. 13-14.

30.   Robert Burns, *Green Grow the Rashes*, stanza 5.

31.   Alexander Pope, "January and May," 11, 59-64.

32.   Stanton, *The Woman's Bible*, p. 19.

33.   Phyllis Trible, "Depatriarchalizing in Biblical Interpretation," *Journal of the American Academy of Religion*, 41 (1973), pp. 36, 40.

34.   Samuel Terrien, "Toward a Biblical Theology of Womanhood," *Religion in Life*, (October 1973), pp. 325, 327.

35.   George Tavard, *Woman in Christian Tradition* (Notre Dame: University Press, 1973), pp. 7-8.

36.   Elizabeth Davis, *The First Sex* (Baltimore: Penguin, 1972), pp. 142-144.

37.   Mary Daly, *Beyond God the Father* (Boston: Beacon Press, 1973), p. 195.

38.   Ibid., p. 95.

39.   Angelina Grimke, *Letters to Catherine Beecher* (Boston, 1836), Letter 12.

40.   Charles Wesley, *Short Hymns on Select Passages of the Holy Scripture* (Bristol, 1762), Vol. I, p. 5. In the twelfth century, Peter Lombard wrote: "Eve was not taken from the feet of Adam to be his slave, nor from his head to be his lord, but from his side to be his partner." (*Sentences* 1, 2, 18)

41.   Reik, *The Creation of Woman*, p. 18.

42. Katharine Rogers, *The Troublesome Helpmate* (Seattle: Univ. of Washington, 1966), pp. 3-4.

43. Phyllis Bird, "Images of Women in the Old Testament," in Rosemary Ruether, ed., *Religion and Sexism* (New York: Simon and Schuster, 1974), p. 72.

44. Mary Hayter, *The New Eve in Christ* (Grand Rapids: Eerdmans, 1987), pp. 97, 114.

45. 1 Peter 3:7.

46. Psalm 146:5.

47. Ernest Lussier, *"Adam* in Gen. 1,1-4, 24," *Catholic Biblical Quarterly*, 18 (1956), pp. 137-139.

48. Mark 10:2-9.

CHAPTER 3: EVE AND PANDORA

1. E.g., Louis Sechan, "Pandore, l'Eve grecque," *Bulletin de l'Association Guillaume Bude* 23 (1929), pp. 3-36; Patricia Marquardt, "Hesiod's Ambiguous View of Women," *Classical Philology* 77 (1982), p. 286; Michael Grant, *Myths of the Greeks and Romans* (New York: World Publishing Co., 1962), p. 124; "Prometheus," *The Oxford Classical Dictionary* (Oxford: Clarendon, 1970); Mark Morford and Robert Lenardon, *Classical Mythology* (New York: Longman, 1985), p. 56.

2. J. E. Bruno, *God as Woman, Woman as God* (New York: Paulist, 1973), p. 21.

3. Walter Headlam, "Prometheus and the Garden of Eden," *Classical Quarterly* 28 (1934), pp. 63-67.

4. Frederick Teggart, "The Argument of Hesiod's *Works and Days*," *Journal of History of Ideas* 8 (1947), p. 50.

5. Gerhard von Rad, *Genesis* (Philadelphia: Westminster Press, 1961), pp. 87-88.

6. Migne, *Patrologia Graeca*, Vol. 89, col. 1013 as translated by Jean Higgins, "Anastasius Sinaita and the Superiority of the Woman," *Journal of Biblical Literature* 97 (1978), p. 254.

7. Jean Higgins, "The Myth of Eve: The Temptress," *Journal of the American Academy of Religion*, 44 (1976),

pp. 646-647.

8. Phyllis Bird, "Images of Women in the Old Testament," in Rosemary Ruether, ed., *Religion and Sexism* (New York: Simon and Schuster, 1974), p. 74.

9. Tikva Frymer–Kensky, "Women," in Paul Achtemeier, ed., *Harper's Bible Dictionary* (San Francisco: Harper & Row, 1985), p. 1140.

10. See P. Walcot, *Hesiod and the Near East* (Cardiff: Wales University Press, 1966), pp. 71-79.

11. A. H. Smith, "The Making of Pandora," *Journal of Hellenic Studies* 11 (1890), p. 283.

12. Aristophanes, *Birds* 972; Philostratus, *Life of Apollonius* 6, 39.

13. T. A. Sinclair, ed., *Hesiod: Works and Days* (London: Macmillan, 1932), p. 12.

14. Robert Graves, *The Greek Myths* (New York: George Braziller, 1955), p. 148.

15. Jane Harrison, *Prolegomena to the Study of Greek Religion* (New York: Arno Press, 1975), pp. 283-285.

16. Hesiod, *Works and Days* 47-105, 373-375; *Theogony* 507-616.

17. *Harvard Studies in Classical Philology* 75 (1971), p. 221.

18. Homer, *Odyssey* 11, 456; 24, 201-202.

19. Sinclair, *Hesiod*, p. xxxvi.

20. Semonides, *On Women* frag. 7.

21. Eva Cantarella, *Pandora's Daughters* (Baltimore: Johns Hopkins, 1987), pp. 69, 177.

22. Eubulus, fr. 116, 117; cf. Mary Lefkowitz and Maureen Fant, *Women's Life in Greece and Rome* (Baltimore: Johns Hopkins, 1982), p. 18.

23. Pherecrates, fr. 248a; Eva Keuls, *The Reign of the Phallus* (New York: Harper & Row, 1985), p. 130.

24. Philo, *Questions and Answers on Genesis* 1, 43 and 45.

25. *The Life of Adam and Eve* 21.

26. Ibid., 11.

27. *Shabbath* 2, 5b, 34.

28. Dora and Erwin Panofsky, *Pandora's Box* (New York: Pantheon, 1962), p. 11.

29. Tertullian, *The Chaplet* 7.

30. Tertullian, *On the Apparel of Women* 1, 1.

31. Paul Jewett, *Man as Male and Female* (Grand Rapids: Eerdmans, 1975), p. 156.

32. John Phillips, *Eve* (San Francisco: Harper & Row, 1984), p. 58.

33. Tertullian, *On the Apparel of Women* 2, 2.

34. Tertullian, *On the Veiling of Virgins* 15.

35. Tertullian, *On the Apparel of Women* 2, 13.

36. John Chrysostom, *Sermons on First Corinthians* 26,3; *Sermons on the Statues* 15, 9.

37. John Chrysostom, *In Matthaeum Homilia* 33, Migne, *Patrologie Graecae*, Vol. 56, col. 803; Heinrich Kramer and James Sprenger, *Malleus Maleficarum* (New York, 1971), pp. 43-47.

38. Gregory Nazianzen, *Oration on the Death of His Father* 8.

39. The painting is in the Louvre museum of Paris; reproduced in Phillips, *Eve*, p. 22.

40. Quoted in Panofsky, *Pandora's Box*, p. 155.

41. John Milton, *The Doctrine and Discipline of Divorce* 2, 3.

42. John Milton, *Paradise Lost* 4, 714-715, 717-719.

43. Quoted in Theodore Reik, *Myth and Guilt* (New York: Braziller, 1970), p. 114.

44. Philip Wylie, *Generation of Vipers* (New York: Pocket Books, 1959), p. 205.

45. Geoffrey Ashe, *The Virgin* (London: Routledge and Kegan Paul, 1976), pp. 16-17.

46. Nikos Kazantzakis, *Zorba the Greek* (New York: Simon and Schuster, 1965), p. 131.

47. Bruce Vawter, *On Genesis* (New York: Doubleday, 1977), p. 87.

48. Elizabeth Stanton, ed., *The Woman's Bible* (New York:

European Pub. Co., 1895), p. 27.

CHAPTER 4: THE FALL AND WOMAN

1. *Apostolic Constitutions* 3, 9.
2. George Riggan, *Original Sin in the Thought of Augustine* (Ann Arbor: University Microfilms, 1970), p. 62.
3. Paul Tillich, *Systematic Theology* (Chicago: Univ. of Chicago Press, 1957), Vol. 2, p. 41.
4. Sirach 25:24; 42:14.
5. Testament of Reuben 5:1-7.
6. Mark 10:2-9.
7. William Phipps, "The Heresiarch: Pelagius or Augustine?" *Anglican Theological Review* (April 1980), pp. 124-133.
8. 1 Tim. 2:12-14 (RSV).
9. Elizabeth Langland and Walter Grove, eds., *A Feminist Perspective in the Academy* (Chicago: Univ. of Chicago Press, 1983), p. 56; cf. Wayne Meeks, "The Image of the Androgyne," *History of Religions* 13 (1974), p. 205.
10. 4 Maccabees 18:8; *Genesis Rabbah* 18; *Sayings of Rabbi Eliezer* 21.
11. Protevangelium of James 13, 1.
12. Justin, *Dialogue with Trypho* 100, 5.
13. Irenaeus, *Against Heresies* 3, 22, 4.
14. John Chrysostom, *Sermons on Timothy* 9.
15. John Chrysostom, *Letters to the Fallen Theodore* 1, 14.
16. Cf. Katharine Rogers, *The Troublesome Helpmate* (Seattle: Univ. of Washington, 1966), pp. 60, 71.
17. Tertullian, *On the Flesh of Christ* 17.
18. Jerome, *Letters* 52, 5.
19. Marina Warner, *Alone of All Her Sex* (New York: Knopf, 1976), p. 58.
20. John Wynn, ed., *Sexual Ethics and Christian Responsibility* (New York: Association Press, 1970), p. 66.
21. "Concupiscence," *New Catholic Encyclopedia* (New York: McGraw-Hill, 1966).

22. Norman P. Williams, *The Ideas of the Fall and of Original Sin* (London: Longmans, Green, 1927), p. 366.

23. Augustine, *City of God* 14, 26.

24. Augustine, *Against Two Letters of the Pelagians* 1, 34.

25. Augustine, *City of God* 14, 24.

26. Ibid., 14, 19.

27. Augustine, *On Original Sin* 39-43.

28. Augustine, *Against Two Letters of the Pelagians* 1, 33.

29. Augustine, *On Marriage and Concupiscence* 1, 7.

30. Augustine, *City of God* 14, 17.

31. Augustine, *Sermons* 151, 5; cf. Peter Brown, *Augustine of Hippo* (Berkeley: Univ. of California, 1969), p. 388.

32. Augustine, *Against Julian* 5, 14.

33. Augustine, *City of God* 14, 18.

34. Augustine, *On Marriage and Concupiscence* 1, 24.

35. Augustine, *City of God* 14, 16.

36. Augustine, *On the Good of Marriage* 11.

37. Augustine, *Sermons* 51, 15.

38. Augustine, *The Sermon on the Mount* 1, 15, 41.

39. Augustine, *On the Good of Marriage* 18.

40. Ibid., 10.

41. Augustine, *On Marriage and Concupiscence* 12; *On Original Sin* 41.

42. Augustine, *On the Good of Marriage* 30.

43. Augustine, *On Marriage and Concupiscence* 2, 14.

44. Augustine, *Unfinished Work Against Julian* 6, 22.

45. Augustine, *City of God* 14, 11.

46. Augustine, *Letters* 243, 10.

47. Augustine, *On the Creed* 10.

48. Augustine, *City of God* 15, 22.

49. David Greene and Frank O'Conner, eds., *A Golden Treasury of Irish Poetry 600-1200* (London: Macmillan, 1967), p. 158.

50. Erich Auerbach, *Mimesis* (New York: Doubleday, 1953), pp. 125-126.

51. Quoted in August Bebel, *Women Against Socialism*

(New York: Labor News Press, 1904), p. 205.

52. Chaucer, *The Canterbury Tale*, 15, 263-64.

53. Chaucer, 6, 275-78.

54. Heinrich Kramer and James Sprenger, *The Malleus Maleficarum* (New York: Dover, 1971), pp. 44, 47.

55. Kramer, p. viii.

56. R. Trevor Davies, *Four Centuries of Witch-Beliefs* (New York: Ayer Co., 1972), p. 4.

57. Ibid., p. 5.

58. See William Phipps, *Influential Theologians on Wo/man* (Washington, D.C.: University Press of America, 1980), pp. 85-95.

59. Augustine, *Against Faustus* 22.

60. John Knox, *The First Blast* (Geneva, 1558), p. 21.

61. T. A. Gill, ed., *The Sermons of John Donne* (New York: Meridian, 1958), pp. 39-47.

62. Erasmus, *Enchiridion Militis Christiani*.

63. "The Divine Truth," *Vital Speeches*, Vol. 34, p. 611.

64. R. F. Trevett, *The Church and Sex* (New York: Hawthorn Books, 1960), pp. 13, 15.

65. *The Westminster Confession* 6, 2-4.

66. From data collected by George Betts in 1928 and by Dean Hoge and John Dyble in 1978. The latter survey from several Lutheran denominations displays that 81 percent believe in total depravity. For some of the results of this study see Hoge and Dyble, "The Influence of Assimilation on American Protestant Ministers' Beliefs, 1928-1978," *Journal for the Scientific Study of Religion* 20 (1981), pp. 64-77.

67. S. H. Kellogg, *The Expositor's Bible: The Book of Leviticus* (New York: Armstrong, 1903), pp. 314, 323-324.

68. Charlotte Gilman, *His Religion and Hers* (New York: Century Co., 1923), p. 44.

69. *Divine Principle* (New York: Unification Press, 1977), p. 89.

70. Ibid., pp. 241-242, 290.

71. Mary Daly, *Beyond God the Father* (Boston: Beacon Press, 1973), p. 44.

72.   John Phillips, *Eve* (San Francisco: Harper & Row, 1984), pp. xiii, 170.

73.   *The Christian Century*, July 18-25, 1984, pp. 701-702 and November 7, 1984, pp. 1,038-1,040.

74.   Paul Ricoeur, *The Symbolism of Evil* (Boston: Beacon Press, 1969), p. 239.

75.   Harry Overstreet, *The Mature Mind* (New York: Norton, 1949), pp. 261, 264.

CHAPTER 5: JESUS AND CREATION

1.   Prov. 3:13-18; 8:22-30.

2.   Wisdom of Solomon 7:25-8:1.

3.   1 Cor. 1:24.

4.   Luke 7:35.

5.   Luke 13:34.

6.   Luke 7:37 (RSV).

7.   Josephus, *Against Apion* 2, 24; Josephus, *Life* 2; cf. William Phipps, *Was Jesus Married*? (Washington: University Press of America, 1986), pp. 55-57.

8.   Origen, *Commentary on John* 2, 12.

9.   Job 33:4.

10.   Odes of Solomon 19:4; 36:1.

11.   *Gospel of Philip* 60.

12.   *Gospel of Philip* 17.

13.   John 14:26.

14.   Quoted in Elisabeth Moltmann-Wendel and Jurgen Moltmann, *Humanity of God* (New York: Pilgrim Press, 1983), p. 103.

15.   Psalm 103:13.

16.   Letha Scanzoni and Nancy Hardesty, *All We're Meant to Be* (Waco, TX: Word Books, 1974), p. 20.

17.   Augustine, *On the Trinity* 12, 5.

18.   *Pastoral Constitution of the Church in the Modern World* 38.

19.   *Westminster Confession of Faith* 9.

20.   Mishnah, *Sotah* 1, 5-6.

21.   *Sotah* 3, 4; Num. 5:16, 24, 27.

22.   John 8:7 (RSV).

23.   Matt. 25:1-3; Luke 13:21, 15:8-10, 18:1-5.

24.   Luke 19:2-10, 21:1-4.

25.   Mark 12:40 (RSV).

26.   Harry E. Fosdick, *The Man from Nazareth* (New York: Harper, 1949), p. 148.

27.   Dorothy Sayers, *Are Women Human?* (Grand Rapids: Eerdmans, 1971), p. 47.

28.   Matt. 19:3 (RSV).

29.   Deut. 24:1 (RSV).

30.   *Gettin* 9, 10.

31.   *Yebamoth* 14, 1.

32.   A. E. Cowley, ed., *Aramaic Papyri of the Fifth Century B. C.* (Oxford, 1923), p. 46.

33.   Sirach 25:26.

34.   Philo, *On the Special Laws* 3, 30, 35.

35.   Josephus, *Life* 414-415, 426-427; cf. *Antiquities* 4, 253.

36.   *Gettin* 9, 10.

37.   Josephus, *Antiquities* 18, 5, 1.

38.   Mark 6:17-29.

39.   Mark 10:2-9.

40.   E.g., Ezek. 44:9; Lev. 25:49; Gen. 6:3; cf. E. D. Burton, *Spirit, Soul, and Flesh* (Chicago, 1918), pp. 68-70.

41.   John 17:20 (RSV).

42.   Eph. 5:31-32.

43.   Cf. Mal. 2:14.

44.   Shakespeare, Sonnet 116.

45.   George F. Moore, *Judaism in the First Centuries of the Christian Era* (Cambridge: Harvard Univ. Press, 1927), Vol. 2, pp. 125, 152.

46.   *Genesis Rabbah* 68, 4.

47.   Israel Abrahams, "Marriages are Made in Heaven," *Jewish Quarterly Review* 2 (1890), p. 173.

48.   Col. 1:15 (RSV).

49.   Aristotle, *Metaphysics* 986a.

50.   Euripides, *Andromache* 181; *Phoenician Maidens* 197.

51.   Philo, *On the Creation* 165.

52.   S. Freud, "Lecture on Femininity" (1938).

53.   E. Fromm, *The Art of Loving* (New York: Bantam, 1963), pp. 31, 35.

54.   E. Brunner, *Man in Revolt* (Philadelphia: Westminister Press, 1947), pp. 352-354.

55.   D. H. Parker, ed., *Schopenhauer Selections* (New York: Scribner's, 1928), p. 427.

56.   Luke 10:33; 15:20; Mark 1:41; 6:34; 8:2; Matt. 20:34.

57.   Luke 7:13.

58.   Aristotle, *History of Animals* 608b.

59.   Shakespeare, *Henry VIII* 3, 2, 428; *Macbeth* 4, 3, 230.

60.   Judges 14:17.

61.   E.g., Gen. 23:2; 29:11; 45:15; 1 Sam. 24:16; 2 Kings 20:3; Job 16:16.

62.   Jer. 9:1 (NEB).

63.   John 11:35 (RSV).

64.   Heb. 5:7 (NEB).

65.   1 Sam. 20:41; 30:4, 2 Sam. 1:12; 3:32; 12:21; 13:36; 15:30; 18:33.

66.   H. T. Lehmann, ed., *Luther's Works* (Philadelphia: Fortress Press, 1967), Tabletalk #55.

67.   Luke 13:34.

68.   Mark 9:36-37.

69.   Matt. 21:15-16; Ps. 8:2.

70.   Lord Chesterfield, Letters, September 5, 1748.

71.   Matt. 18:1-4 (RSV).

72.   Luke 23:46; Ps. 31:5; Talmud, *Berakot* 5a.

73.   Matt. 11:28-29 (Good News).

74.   John 8:1-11.

75.   2 Cor. 10:1 (Good News).

76.   Mary C. Davies, "Door-Mats," in B. Stevenson, ed., *The Home Book of Quotations* (New York: Dodd, Mead & Co., 1944), p. 2,178.

77. Mark 10:45; John 13:5.
78. Cf. 1 Sam. 25:41.
79. Prov. 31:20 (NEB).
80. Acts 10:38.
81. Gen. 3:16.
82. Mark 8:31.
83. John 16:21.
84. A. E. Garvie, "Womanliness," *Dictionary of Christ in the Gospels* (New York: Scribner's, 1908).
85. Aristotle, *Politics* 1,254b-1,260a.
86. E.g., Mark 1:16-22.
87. Mark 4:35-41.
88. Matt. 8:20.
89. Mark 8:27-9:8.
90. Matt. 23.
91. Mark 11:15-19.
92. John 18:37; 19:10-11.
93. E.g., Matt. 5:21-48; 7:28-29; Mark 2:23-3:4; John 4:7-26.
94. Luke 20:26.
95. Moltmann, *Humanity in God*, p. 38.
96. Rosemary Ruether, "The Sexuality of Jesus," *Christianity and Crisis*, May 29, 1978, p. 136.
97. Luke 24:19; John 1:30; Acts 2:22.
98. Phil. 2:7-8.
99. Rom. 5:15.
100. John 7:46.
101. John 19:5.
102. John 8:40.
103. Origen, *Matthew Homilies* 10, 17; Janet Crawford and Michael Kinnamon, eds., *In God's Image* (Geneva: World Council of Churches, 1983), p. 26.
104. Sarah Grimke, *Letters on Equality* (Boston, 1832), p. 18.
105. Col. 3:12.
106. Theodore Roszak, *Masculine/Feminine* (New York:

Harper & Row, 1969), p. 102.
107. "Campaign Teardrops," *Time* March 13, 1972; cf. *New York Times* March 5, 1972, p. 33.
108. Carolyn Heilbrun, *Toward a Recognition of Androgyny* (New York: Knopf, 1973), p. xvi.

CHAPTER 6: PARADISE CONTINUED

1. Omar Khayyam, *Rubaiyat* 45-49.
2. Song of Songs 4:11, 13.
3. Isa. 11:7.
4. Samuel Terrien, *Till the Heart Sings* (Philadelphia: Fortress, 1985), p. 16.
5. Francis Landy, "The Song of Songs and the Garden of Eden," *Journal of Biblical Literature* 98 (1979), pp. 513, 528.
6. Song of Songs 2:13 (RSV).
7. Song of Songs 2:3; 4:13; 7:8.
8. Song of Songs 4:14.
9. Song of Songs 1:16-17 (RSV).
10. Song of Songs 4:15.
11. Song of Songs 2:10-12.
12. Song of Songs 1:6-8.
13. Song of Songs 2:17.
14. Song of Songs 4:1, 5.
15. Song of Songs 3:4.
16. Mishnah, *Sotah* 9, 14.
17. Song of Songs 3:11.
18. Song of Songs 6:13.
19. Song of Songs 1:4.
20. Song of Songs 8:12; 1 Kings 11:3 (RSV).
21. Song of Songs 6:9 (RSV).
22. Song of Songs 2:1-2.
23. Song of Songs 1:2.
24. Song of Songs 5:10-16.
25. Song of Songs 7:1-9.
26. Michael Fox, "Love, Passion, and Perception in Is-

raelite and Egyptian Love Poetry," *Journal of Biblical Literature* 102 (1983), p. 228.

27.   Phyllis Trible, "Depatriarchalizing in Biblical Interpretation," *Journal of the American Academy of Religion* 41 (1973), p. 47; Trible has expanded her interpretation of the equality and mutuality motifs of the Song of Songs in *God and the Rhetoric of Sexuality* (Philadelphia: Fortress, 1978), pp. 144-165.

28.   Song of Songs 8:9-10.

29.   Song of Songs 2:7; 3:5; 8:4.

30.   Song of Songs 4:12 (RSV).

31.   Song of Songs 4:16.

32.   Song of Songs 8:6-7.

33.   Jacquetta Hawkes, *The First Great Civilization* (New York: Knopf, 1973), p. 177.

34.   Theophile J. Meek, "Babylonian Parallels to the Song of Songs," *Journal of Biblical Literature* 43 (1924), pp. 245-252.

35.   John B. White, *A Study of the Language of Love in the Song of Songs and Ancient Egyptian Poetry* (Missoula, Montana: Scholars Press, 1978).

36.   Quoted in Vern Bullough, *The Subordinate Sex* (Baltimore: Penguin, 1974), pp. 39-40.

37.   Mary Lefkowitz and Maureen Fant, eds., *Women's Life in Greece and Rome* (Baltimore: Johns Hopkins, 1982), pp. 3-6.

38.   Mishnah, *Yadaim* 3, 5.

39.   Prov. 5:18-19.

40.   *Ketubot* 62b.

41.   William Phipps, "The Plight of the Song of Songs," *Journal of the American Academy of Religion* 42 (1974), pp. 82-100.

42.   Denis de Rougemont, *Love in the Western World* (New York: Pantheon, 1956), pp. 316-318.

43.   Friedrich Engels, *The Origin of the Family* (Chicago: Kerr's, 1902), p. 84.

44.   Dietrich Bonhoeffer, *Letters and Papers from Prison*

(New York: Macmillan, 1972), p. 303.

45.   Viktor Frankl, *Man's Search for Meaning* (New York: Washington Square Press, 1963), pp. 58, 61.

46.   Karl Barth, *Church Dogmatics* (Edinburgh: Clark, 1958-59), Vol. 3/1, pp. 312-329; 3/2, pp. 291-300.

47.   Alan Watts, *Beyond Theology* (New York: Pantheon, 1964), p. 174.

48.   Helmut Gollwitzer, *Song of Love* (Philadelphia: Fortress, 1979), p. 26.

Selected Bibliography

Eliade, Mircea. *The Two and the One*. London: Harvill, 1965.

Hayter, Mary, *The New Eve in Christ*. Grand Rapids: Eerdmans, 1987.

Panofsky, Doris and Erwin. *Pandora's Box*. New York: Pantheon, 1962.

Phillips, John. *Eve: The History of an Idea*. San Francisco: Harper & Row, 1984.

Phipps, William. *Influential Theologians on Wo/Man*. Washington, DC: University Press of America, 1980.

Stanton, Elizabeth, ed. *The Woman's Bible*. New York: European Publishing Co., 1895. Reissued by Arno Press, 1974.

Swidler, Leonard. *Biblical Affirmation of Woman*. Philadelphia: Westminster, 1979.

Terrien, Samuel. *Till the Heart Sings*. Philadelphia: Fortress, 1985.

Trible, Phyllis. *God and the Rhetoric of Sexuality*. Philadelphia: Fortress, 1978.

Index

ABOUT THE AUTHOR

BILL PHIPPS has spent most of his career teaching at a liberal arts college in West Virginia. He is Professor of Religion and Philosophy and Chairman of the Department of Religion and Philosophy at Davis and Elkins College. He is a graduate of Davidson College and Union Theological Seminary in Virginia. He received his Ph.D. in biblical interpretation from the University of St. Andrews in Scotland.

Dr. Phipps's writings over the past two decades have focused on the relationship between religion and sexuality. Among his books are *Was Jesus Married?* and *Recovering Biblical Sensuousness*. His articles on this topic have been published in the *New York Times*, the *Journal of the American Academy of Religion*, *Christian Century*, *Theology Today*, *Pastoral Psychology*, *Presbyterian Survey*, *Journal of Religion and Health*, *Journal of Ecumenical Studies*, *New Testament Studies*, and *Studies in Religion*.